ALMUT BOCKEMÜHL was born in 1933 in Idar-Oberstein, Germany. She studied German literature and biology and, as the mother of four children, made an intensive study of fairy tales and folk tales. She is a freelance writer, lecturer and course leader, and lives in Dornach, Switzerland.

GH00457960

A Woman's Path

Motherhood, Love and Personal Development

Almut Bockemühl

Sophia Books

Sophia Books
Hillside House, The Square
Forest Row, RH18 5ES

www.rudolfsteinerpress.com

Published by Sophia Books 2009
An imprint of Rudolf Steiner Press

Originally published in German under the title *Selbstfindung und Muttersein im Leben der Frau* in 1989 by Verlag Freies Geistesleben, Stuttgart. Translated from German by Pauline Wehrle, based on the 3rd revised edition, 1994, with additional editing by Matthew Barton

A catalogue record for this book is available from the British Library

ISBN 978 1 85584 214 4

Cover by Andrew Morgan Design.
Cover photo © Michael Damkier, fotolia.com
Typeset by DP Photosetting, Neath, West Glamorgan
Printed and bound in Malta by Gutenberg Press Ltd.

Mixed Sources
Product group from well-managed forests, and other controlled sources
www.fsc.org Cert no. TT-CoC-002424
© 1996 Forest Stewardship Council

FSC

The paper used for this book is FSC-certified and totally chlorine-free. FSC (the Forest Stewardship Council) is an international network to promote responsible management of the world's forests.

Contents

Preface

'Could you write a book about a mother's vocation that has fundamental things to say yet also springs from personal experience? Nowadays it seems that bringing up children really needs to be tackled consciously if it is to be successful in future.'

This question immediately set something stirring in me. Millions of women, surely, face the problem of how to integrate motherhood with their own deepest, personal aims? And on the other hand, isn't bringing up children just as meaningful and fulfilling a vocation as any other?

I hesitated to take up the challenge at once, however. With a natural desire for children but by no means a love of housework, I had already reared four children and then resumed a mothering role by caring for old people over many years. I therefore thought I had done my duty as far as tending others was concerned, and could now devote the rest of my life to the personal interests I had left to one side since my student days—such as literature, poetry and language. However, I also realized that writing about motherhood and family life in a positive light would mean that many readers, particularly women, would inevitably dismiss it as 'old-fashioned'. Time and again we hear women speaking of the 'lost years' they have devoted to their children. This is a sign of inner discord and dissatisfaction that cannot be overcome in outer ways, but solely from within—by changing our attitude to circumstances. A woman today should not have to lead two separate, sundered lives. Instead, by connecting fully with every activity she engages in, she can integrate it with her personality. In other words, the woman who is mother of a large family is the same person as the woman who engages in artistic or intellectual pursuits.

As a child I was passionately fond of playing on a swing—an image that for me has come to symbolize my own circumstances and those of countless other women. A swing first goes as far as it can in one direction—but not indefinitely. Its original impetus is balanced and counteracted by an opposite impetus. For this to happen, however, it has to be supported at one point, and this pivotal point has to be at rest.

The swing's movements are our activities, and the pivot is our calm ego or 'I' that sets the motion going, and on which the movement works back in turn. Can these movements become our own initiative, or are we merely sent hither and thither at the mercy of circumstance?

Swinging or rocking also happens to be an ancient, archetypal activity. The Greeks, Romans and Slavs had rocking festivals in the spring when winter and summer were poised in equilibrium—the woods turning green, and the weather growing milder. In the rites of Dionysus, rocking was used in fertility magic and to drive out demons. We also read of ancient funeral rites where the corpse of a person who had committed suicide was rocked to propitiate the gods. Someone who had fallen out of equilibrium by breaking a fundamental law was thus brought back into rhythm by rocking the corpse. Rocking is a rhythmic movement that reconciles opposites.[1]

A woman who wishes simultaneously to find herself as an individual and to devote herself to motherhood is caught between two extremes that are hard to reconcile. No hard-and-fast rules apply, and all one can do is describe one's personal experiences, and pass on thoughts and views. In my case this would have been inconceivable without the help I drew from a lifelong involvement with Rudolf Steiner's anthroposophy. In anthroposophical spiritual science the aim is 'to cultivate the life of the soul, both in the individual and in human society, based on a true knowledge of the world of spirit'.[2] I cannot imagine my life without this aim. However this book is by no means an introduction to anthroposophy, nor does it aim to educate or advise. There are enough self-help books of this kind already, and I have no wish to add to them.

I have tried instead to give many examples and to stick as closely as possible to actual experience. The book will thus be a very personal one, despite including general—and in all cases incomplete—observations and historical references. These serve only to illuminate my perspective.

My 33-year marriage and bringing up my children are the experiences underlying what I have to say. There is a subtle reproach in the way people sometimes stress how well the women of my generation performed their duty as mothers and wives, without breaking out of existing norms. The underlying biographical reality, however, is that my generation grew up during the war years. At a very impressionable age we experienced families being fragmented and brutally torn apart. In those days only the mothers brought the children up. And after the war it was a common, very painful experience to see fathers gradually returning to other families but not to one's own. A sense arose in consequence that this is not how life should be, nurturing a determination to do everything possible to ensure that one's own children grow up in a 'real' family. At the same time this gave my generation insight into what it means for a woman to cope on her own with her children, and survive.

This is the thread connecting my book to the past. On the other hand the succeeding generation—my children and their friends—have confronted me with problems, mostly psychological in nature, of which we would never have dreamed in our day. We took many things for granted which are now questioned. Such problems often arise in a radical way before a partnership has even been established.

I have repeatedly discussed all these questions in conversations with a wide range of friends, both female and male. A number of people have worked though the manuscript and made comments. I should like to give my warmest thanks to all of them and also to my dear husband, my three sons, Cornelis, Olaf and Laurens, and especially my daughter, Erdmuthe.

The Women's Movement

> Women are especially called upon today to find and
> assert themselves. Everything that happens in this
> direction will be of benefit to humanity.[3]
>
> *Rudolf Steiner*

If you take stock of yourself as a woman and a mother, or talk
to other women about how they relate to their children,
husband and profession, and how they feel about these
relationships, you notice time and again that many problems
that used to exist have ceased to be problems, whereas
questions and situations have now arisen that we would not
have dreamed of in the past. The way people live with and
relate to one another has changed in the course of the past
century to an unprecedented extent. It is impossible to give a
picture of all these changes, but we can certainly point to
some of the underlying tendencies.

At the end of the nineteenth century the structures of
society suddenly started entering into greater turmoil and
flux. Both the youth movement and the women's movement
are clear signs of the advent of a new age. People began to
question basic aspects of society, and cast doubt on traditions
and authorities. Women who had been completely taken up
in serving their families began to find their own identity.

Around the beginning of the twentieth century, significant
individual women appeared on the cultural horizon and
vigorously pursued their own path. I could name numerous
examples. Some of them carved out a career for themselves

by studying at university—which was fraught with difficulties in those days. The writer Ricarda Huch (1864–1947) was one of the first German women to obtain a degree. Maria Montessori (1870–1952), the first woman medical student in Rome, became well known later for her teaching methods for children with learning difficulties. Marie Curie (1867–1934), who discovered radium, struggled against great odds to study in Paris. Other women searched for new and unconventional approaches to art—for instance Isadora Duncan (1878–1927), with her very expressive art of movement based on the classical era, or the Jewish lyrical poet Elsa Lasker-Schüler (1869–1945). The lives of both these women were like one long protest against traditional bourgeois culture, making their circumstances extremely fraught and complex.

Particularly tragic are biographies such as that of Franziska von Reventlow (1871–1918) who, only moderately gifted artistically, led a life of 'free love' among the artistic circles of Swabia. This eventually led to her inability either to form a lasting relationship or to have a solid professional career. This was an escape from the status quo without being able to find support of a new kind.

Why did such protests against social structures not occur before? On the whole women had for centuries submitted to their allotted tasks. Had they no need, or did they lack the strength to set themselves new goals? It is clear that at the end of the nineteenth century something suddenly became possible that was not so before.

Let us look at circumstances in medieval times. People were connected very strongly with the communities in which they lived, and in those days these were small villages and towns-in-the-making, which we find amazingly easy to survey at one glance if we reconstruct them today. Everyone knew everybody else. The village community belonged together like a family. People were part of their natural and human environment and did not distinguish themselves so strongly from each other.

Life was much more of a public affair, with no separation in our sense between work in the home and professional vocation. Whether they were farmers or craftspeople, both the husband and the wife worked in the vicinity of the home, albeit in clearly allotted roles.

The Church represented spiritual life, to which everyone could and in fact had to belong. Its authority was not questioned initially, any more than were the other hierarchical divisions of society, and the roles people were obliged to take according to their sex.

This questioning began, however, with the religious reform movements of the thirteenth century, irrespective of whether these were sanctioned by the Church or declared heretical. Certain individuals slowly began to step out of the group experience.

An example of a revolutionary who made life extremely uncomfortable for her contemporaries was the Countess Elisabeth of Thüringen (1207–31). Her life was suitably set to rights after her death in that the Church declared her a saint. The radical way in which she, as a daughter of the King of Hungary, practised equality was unheard of in her time. Widowed at the age of 20, she dedicated her life to God without joining any of the existing orders. She took a vow, not via a priest, as was the custom, but directly to God, by laying her hand on the altar. This was her way of showing her independence. The kind of life she established with a small community of like-minded people combined devoted ser-

vice to those in need with an intense spiritual life. This was an
ideal that accorded with the deeply religious nature of the
age, but still seems exemplary in our time.

A personality such as she anticipated an impulse—that of
the free individual—which did not break through in full
force until the Reformation.

Individuals achieve strength and certainty through their
own efforts, and in the distinctive way they form their own
life of soul. The monks did their meditative exercises to
strengthen inner life in complete seclusion from the outer
world, which would have been too great a distraction. This
inner spiritual life of thought and feeling reached its peak in
scholasticism and mysticism. People needed to attain this
intense level of inner life to confront afresh the world of the
senses.

Individualized life means being able to distinguish an inner
from an outer world. A kind of image of this process, in
which a 'private' arena of the soul became more and more
pronounced, can be seen in the increasing appearance of
people's private life as something separate from the public
domain. People felt a growing need for a separate sphere, for
domestic life. The family began to develop a life of its own.

For the women, who were more closely bound to the
sphere of domesticity than the men, this signified increased
isolation. The domestication of women really falls in the
period between the sixteenth and the nineteenth centuries.
The patriarchal tendency we hear so much about found its
culmination in the nineteenth century.

If we examine this critically we must not overlook the fact
that the 'pater familias' not only had supreme authority but
also a heavy burden of responsibility for the livelihood of his
family, which depended on him absolutely. There was no

such thing as state social security. If the man as 'bread-winner' died, his wife was left helpless and impoverished. Even if she went out to work she could not support her family, as she was on principle paid less than a man.

In the 'higher' social classes of the eighteenth and nineteenth centuries the helplessness and illiteracy of women was actually exploited. They were intentionally restricted to the domestic sphere. They could often barely read and write, if at all. They were pleasant toys for the men, and their lack of accomplishments only served to enhance their husband's self-importance. This, and the revolt against it, is depicted in Ibsen's play *The Dolls House* (1879).

It was in protest against this sort of situation that the women's civil rights movement arose,[4] fighting first and foremost for education for girls, free access to professional careers, and better pay. This was a real need of the times. Nevertheless the women's movement is misunderstood if one looks only at its outer aspect. It was not solely to do with opportunities to earn more money, nor with proving that women could do professional work as well as men. There was also an inner need for it.

In the Middle Ages, as we have seen, cultural life and religion were identical. From the fifteenth century onwards a purely scientific mode of thought began to develop and to separate off from religion, which thus increasingly lost its significance.

So it came about that in the nineteenth century an inviolate faith in scientific progress suddenly took the place previously occupied by religion. The advancement of science, however, was men's business. Therefore women were excluded from the task of wrestling with the problems of existence—which actually means spiritual endeavour as such.

Women's fight to gain access to the professions and to study was therefore not a practical and financial matter only but a remonstration against their exclusion from cultural life altogether.

This led initially to men beginning to discuss the extent to which women were capable of intellectual achievements or whether it were possible to involve them in public service.

In Meyer's 1905 encyclopaedia, the following paragraph comes under the heading 'Equal status of women':

> The demand for equal political status comes less from a practical need than from a theoretical assumption of doubtful worth. The mind of a woman as well as her prevailing disposition make her seem little suited to active participation in public life.

The section on 'Women studying' contains the passage:

> The assertion made by the opponents of study for women, namely, that the female sex does not have the ability to do independent academic research, is not acceptable. Experience shows that women are capable to an average degree of the demands of professional studies.

Rudolf Steiner's stance on the question of women's rights in his *The Philosophy of Freedom* should be judged against this background:

> As long as men debate whether women 'according to their natural disposition' are suited to this or that profession, no progress will be made in the so-called woman's question. What women are capable of by nature must be left to women to decide. If it is true that women are fit only for the professions that are theirs at present, then they will

hardly have it in them to manage any others. But women must be allowed to decide for themselves what is and what is not in accordance with their nature. To those who fear a social upheaval if women are accepted as individuals rather than as members of their sex, it must be said that a social structure in which the status of half of humanity is beneath human dignity is itself in great need of improvement.[5]

Science was purely intellectual or academic in nature to start with but when, in the nineteenth century, technology appeared on the scene, science entered the domain of practical life. Its aim was no longer seen as exclusively epistemological, but as an enquiry into what could or could not be done practically. Areas that had formerly been in the hands of women—the making of textiles and food production, for instance—were embraced by industrial development and transferred to factories. The machine age began as a clear product of male culture.

Factories are not a pleasant or particularly human environment for anyone, perhaps especially not for women and least of all for children. We know, however, how women and children were exploited in factories and under what oppressive social conditions they lived. Here lies the root of the 'working class women's movement' that existed from the beginning alongside the more well-to-do suffragettes, and was of a quite different character. Whilst middle class women wanted access to the professions, the goal of the working classes was to release women from jobs and set them free for their family. In this case the question of women's rights was not an isolated one but part of the whole labour question.

The fact that women of both the middle and the working

classes experienced constraints and sought change at the same time shows clearly that a new awareness was emerging in Europe that related to the world in a fundamentally different way. Whereas people had formerly been subordinate to nature they now began to assume mastery over it, and exerted a pressure on it that eventually became so great that the very survival of the natural world is now threatened.

The first stage of this new awareness was that people no longer felt *in their world* but separate and distinct from it. We speak in science of 'the external observer'. In the development of this 'onlooker consciousness' and the self-esteem it generates, men have the lead. It may well be that they have acquired this lead through the fact that it was almost always the man's business to tackle an enemy in time of war. Such practice in external confrontation led to the capacity for inner confrontation and detachment as well, which may ultimately be no less destructive.

From the twentieth century onwards it is the special task of the female members of humanity to create a counterbalance to this. This is how one should understand the quotation from Rudolf Steiner that heads this chapter. The women's movement is ultimately women's struggle to develop sufficient self-awareness for this vital task.

Developing the strength and determination to assert oneself has to be looked at to begin with as a masculine drive; therefore we can understand that women began by going in a masculine direction. To overcome their feminine constraints and one-sidedness they endeavoured to conquer areas of life in which men believed they had the sole privilege. This started with externalities. Short hair and trousers gave them a greater feeling of freedom and mobility. No modern woman thinks twice about it now. It seems strange to us to hear what happened to Olympia de Gouges, a pioneer of the women's movement at the time of the French Revolution. After the early success of her demands for 'women's rights' she made bitter enemies when she called for women to wear men's clothes in order to eradicate external distinctions of sex. That was the last straw and she ended on the scaffold.

The so-called 'sexual emancipation of women' in the last century is also based on a masculine trend. It stems from the hypothesis that the sexual needs of women are equal to those of men but have been suppressed up to now through education and social environment.

The sex theories of Sigmund Freud (1856–1939), the founder of psychoanalysis, are conceived entirely from the male point of view and present female sexuality as though women were castrated men. This is how Freud arrives at the idea of women envying men their penis, which is difficult to understand for most normal women. Freud made sexuality the mainspring for just about every human action, starting from infancy. That these opinions took hold the way they did must be due to our materialistic age. His ideas initially spread rapidly in Europe and went on to acquire great importance in America in the 1930s and 40s. We can probably say that the post-war wave of 'sexual liberation' emanating from America was set in motion by this line of thought.

Against this background it is shattering to discover that Freud himself falsified the results of his research for fear of public scandal.[6] He had started his enquiries from the fact that many of his patients who suffered from hysteria reported seduction or sexual abuse in early childhood, often by their own father. This produced a kind of sexual trauma. Because of the icy reception this received among Freud's colleagues he later on dropped the 'seduction theory' and explained his patients' accounts as products of the imagination, developing his 'child sexuality theory'.

It would have been an important mission for the women's liberation movement to pursue the question of child abuse. This proved impossible because 'the seduction theory', which was unfortunately absolutely true and still applies today, was systematically suppressed. Instead, women took energetic hold of another of Freud's ideas: that one should liberate oneself from all inhibiting moral restraints altogether so as to achieve sexual satisfaction.

At the beginning of the twentieth century there was much talk of double standards. The sexual conduct of men on the one hand and women on the other was judged by completely differing standards. Women justifiably opposed this, and crucial changes have occurred in this realm in recent decades. However, women should be fully aware that these changes led to women adapting their moral outlook to those of men, rather than vice versa.

The women's movement must be seen primarily and predominantly as a movement of emancipation: from being tied to the home, from economic disadvantage, male suppression, and restrictions due to sex and conventional morality. At some points, however, this movement has risen above the struggle for personal rights to a universally human level: in the women's peace movement.

A movement of this kind arose at the beginning of the First World War. In September 1914 its representatives handed Wilson, the US President, a peace petition requesting they negotiate between the belligerent countries. A million women of 13 nations signed the resolution. It is interesting that although women are not generally called up for military service they tend more towards pacifism than men. Lida G.

Heyman, who was a leading figure in the women's movement at the beginning of the twentieth century, advocated
the rejection of distinctions between typically female and
typically male attributes with one exception:

> There is one difference between men and women: their
> attitude to creative life. As the source of life a woman
> values the trials inherent in the creation of life very dif-
> ferently from a man . . . therefore women, merely by virtue
> of being women, are the greatest exponents of pacifism.[7]

It is not very well known that a women's peace movement
also existed in Germany after the Second World War. The
Democratic Women's Alliance of Germany[8] was originally
an anti-Fascist resistance movement whose prime goal was
peace, together with democracy and equality. But since only
a few years after the war Adenauer's government was
advocating remilitarization and the integration of West
Germany with the West, this movement, which strongly
opposed the reintroduction of general mobilization, was
vilified, suppressed and finally banned in 1957 as 'anti-
constitutional and dangerous to the state'. At this time the
connecting threads with East Germany were cut in favour of
an alliance with the West, leading to the 'economic miracle'.

The interests of younger women imperceptibly shifted
back to personal problems. The battle for equality continued.
The right to vote and access to professional careers had
already been won in Germany in 1918. In 1949 legal equality
became established as part of the German Constitution, and
in 1958 the law of equal status came into force.

In England, organized suffrage had begun in 1866, and was
supported by some men such as John Stuart Mill. In 1897, 17
of these groups came together to form the National Union of

Women's Suffrage Societies (NUWSS), who held public meetings, wrote letters to politicians and published various texts. In 1907, the NUWSS organized its first large procession. This march became known as the Mud March as over 3000 women trudged through rutted streets of London from Hyde Park to Exeter Hall to call for women's suffrage.

In 1903, a number of members of the NUWSS broke away and, led by Emmeline Pankhurst, formed the Women's Social and Political Union (WSPU). As the national media lost interest in the suffrage campaign, the WSPU decided it would use other methods to create publicity. This began in 1905 when two members of the WSPU kept on heckling in Parliament, calling out, 'Will the Liberal Government give votes to women?' The two suffragettes were arrested and charged with assault after a struggle.

After this media success, the WSPU's tactics became increasingly violent. This included an attempt in 1908 to storm the House of Commons, and an incident in 1913 in which Emily Davison, a suffragette, interfered with a horse owned by King George V during the Epsom Derby, was trampled and died four days later. The WSPU ceased their militant activities during the First World War and agreed to assist the war effort. Similarly, the NUWSS announced that they would cease political activity but continued to lobby discreetly throughout the war. In 1918, with the war over, Parliament agreed to enfranchise women who were over the age of 30. It was not until 1928 with the Representation of the People Act that women were granted the right to vote on the same terms as men.

The so-called 'new women's movement' arose from the anti-authoritarian student movement in the years around 1968. Initially this did not focus on the general social disadvantages of women, but highlighted the fact that male students advocating emancipation from social constraints had, in practice, no intention of altering their behaviour towards their wives and girlfriends. The question under scrutiny was whether only women were really responsible for the children, and should therefore sideline their own personal development. The movement endeavoured to break out of a stereotypical female role. Abortion legislation again became the subject of keen discussion. Breaking the mould of the family and revolutionizing education were at stake.

Part of the women's movement took a radical turn and became neo-feminist. Far from aiming to share dominance with men, this movement wished to supplant them. Through all sorts of projects—women's magazines, women's bookshops, women's publishing companies, women's pubs, women's living quarters—a kind of women's sub-culture arose, even leading to grotesque aberrations such as 'thealogy' (female theology).

Despite all these activities many feminists suffer from a feeling of resignation nowadays because the successes they hoped for are so long in coming. Part of the reason for this is that women are never unanimous about their objectives. But how can it be otherwise in an era when our attitude to life's problems is determined not by our sex but by our individuality?

We can, nevertheless, speak of significant successes extending below the surface of things. As I mentioned at the beginning, the whole mood of life, the whole way women relate to their profession, to marriage and motherhood, has changed tremendously in recent decades. Whether women are basically capable or incapable of professional work or of taking public office is no longer in question. Many women have shown that it is possible to combine a profession with a family. Meanwhile, however, they have also discovered that doing this requires an amount of energy which, due more to psychological than physical stress, is only manageable in the shorter term. Career women often have a guilty conscience, somehow, where their children are concerned. Thus there is currently a trend to return to the home. Betty Friedan, whose book *The Feminine Mystique* caused quite a commotion in America when it appeared, is now speaking of the 'second stage' in which the role of the family in the life of society is re-examined and accentuated.[9]

It would be impossible, of course, to go back to the old ways. The movement of 1968 really has done away to a large extent with traditions, conventions, middle-class morals and religious principles relating to marriage and the family that still obtained in the 1950s. Families were ripe for destruction. And they *were* destroyed inasmuch as the majority of pupils in a class now often come from broken families. We cannot take anything for granted any longer in the social realm; everything has to be renewed. Every individual person obviously still retains from his or her upbringing a number of unreflective ways of behaving. These combine chaotically with arbitrary ideas and suggestive models drawn from psychology, the latter assuming the authority which religion once had.

External freedoms have been created: people can live together whether they are married or not; men can wear their hair long; we can go to the theatre wearing anything we like. Yet it is increasingly obvious that real freedom is an inner matter. If someone has not achieved inner freedom then the jeans fashion is just as restrictive as evening dress or a bowler hat, living together without being married is just as unin-

spiring as our grandparents' marriage, and the alternative way
of life becomes just another norm.

Today's social chaos is a tremendous challenge. Its
uncertainties can give rise to new forms if we seize the
opportunity. This is not a matter for women only but for the
whole of humanity. Nothing has sustaining power any longer
if it is simply adopted from the past. Nevertheless we cannot
just behave as though the world began with us. We need an
awareness of our historical past to understand our own
position in the stream of evolution and human development.

Ileana Simziana

There is a Russian fairy tale about a princess who puts on male
attire and fights for the Emperor because her father has no son.
The Emperor gives her the hardest tasks, all of which she
accomplishes. She even fetches him Ileana Simziana, the most
beautiful of beauties. However, when it comes to the next task
of fetching the christening font from the other side of the
Jordan, the hermit keeping vigil over it curses her with the
words: 'If you are a man, become a woman! If you are a woman,
become a man!' And she undergoes a sex change.

'He' returns home and, after the death of the Emperor, Ileana
Simziana wants to marry her beautiful liberator. He accepts her,
saying: 'As you have chosen me I will have you. But I warn you
that in my house the cock crows and not the hen!'

This may act as a caution to us to ensure that our endeavours
at emancipation do not lead to the donning of masculine garb
and the overlaying of our inherent nature.

The Desecration of Nature

Astonishing, the caution of human gesture
on Attic stelae. Love and parting so lightly
laid upon shoulders as though made of a fabric
finer than ours. Just think of the hands
resting weightless, despite the torsos' strength.
Their mastery knew: that's as far as we go—
to touch one another like this; the gods
press down more powerfully upon us. But that's for
   the gods.[10]

Rainer Maria Rilke

Never before in the history of humanity has the human body
been so divested of soul and spirit as over the past century.
Any colour supplement will show the lack of scruples we
now have about nudity. And this is not a sign of being particularly natural, but a reaction against centuries of hostility
from the Church to the sensory, material world, and its view
of the body as the seat of the devil. Ethnic tribes, like the
ancient Greeks, still had a 'childlike' connection with their
own body. No adult in our civilization can display his or her
body as naturally as a child can, for to some extent this
requires the innocence of paradise. Little children often do
not notice sexual characteristics or, for instance, the changes
their mother's body goes through during pregnancy, unless
someone particularly draws their attention to it.

According to the legend of paradise it was not until after
the 'Fall' that Adam and Eve saw that they were naked,
which means they awoke at that moment to a clearer form of

consciousness and became more aware of themselves. Until then they were clothed by the 'aura' of their spiritual being, which primitive humanity could perceive clairvoyantly. Although people of ancient cultures had already left paradise, they still had a strong experience of the soul qualities that their body emanated. Dress imitates these, thus pointing us to the original meaning of clothing.

It is only when we regard the physical realm as inter-penetrated by spirit that we can understand ancient customs, which even made sexual surrender a sacrificial service to the gods—so-called religious prostitution. Personal interests played no part in this. A soul relationship to the priest who performed the sexual act was permitted neither before nor afterwards. This sexual temple worship took place in a state of dimmed consciousness, as a sacrifice to the gods. It was a kind of surrender whereby a woman felt released from separate existence and received into the world of the gods.

On the other hand, from very early times onwards, people used sexual abstinence as a means of increasing spiritual potency, and this played a great part in the Christian Middle Ages. It was known that forces are expended in sexuality that can also be 'saved up' and made use of in other realms.

Tacitus (c. 55–120) reports on ancient mystery customs on the peninsular of Jutland. Among the Germanic tribes living there sexual union was allowed to take place only during a set time in the spring in connection with rites dedicated to the goddess Nerthus.

In a lecture on 21 December 1916, Rudolf Steiner spoke further about this report by Tacitus:[11]

The characteristic strength at which—even in its after-math—Tacitus marvelled, when he wrote a century after

the Mystery of Golgotha, was due to the fact that the
forces, which enter into such sexual union, were, through
abstinence, preserved during the whole of the rest of the
year and flowed instead into physical strength.

At these festivals an image of the goddess was borne in a
chariot drawn by cows. When the rites were over the goddess, 'weary of her sojourn among mortals', was taken back to
her shrine. Thereupon the chariot, the veil and the goddess
herself were immersed in a hidden lake. The slaves who
carried out this service were drowned immediately afterwards, so that all knowledge of these things would sink down
into the night of the subconscious. The people who celebrated their marriage at this festival experienced conception
in a kind of dream annunciation. The sacredness of the
proceeding was not to be spoilt by profane day consciousness.

One has to realize that in these ancient times, in general,
sexual union took place in a greatly dimmed state of consciousness, 'in sleep'. The expression 'sleeping together'
indicates this.

The biblical description of 'the immaculate conception'
must also be understood in this light. We are not being told
of a biological impossibility (for Joseph is expressly named as
the father of Jesus) but of a process that was completely
hidden from Mary's waking consciousness, one that was
normal in ancient times and in this case, exceptionally,
reoccurred. Mary learned from the angel's annunciation that
she had conceived. That is, she perceived an occurrence,
which was the spiritual counterpart of physical conception.

When white men discovered native Australians they were
amazed to find that the aboriginals imagined that, for conception to take place, a man had to dream a child's soul. At

the same time he also had to receive its name and pass this on to his wife. As the Europeans were not told any more than this they initially believed that the Australians did not know how children were really conceived. In actual fact these people still lived in a primitive condition of pictorial consciousness, which nowadays we only find in children in our civilization.

In ancient civilizations people knew that the forces working through reproduction are very powerful, creative forces of life. To disclose and tamper with these mysteries was a punishable offence. This is why the entry into this realm was often connected with severe tests of will-power. Ulrich Mann has written an article on the Cretan 'bull games' of Minoan civilization, that is, during the third millennium BC. The trial was as follows. Before their first sexual union the descendants of the royal house had to undergo a trial, which involved vaulting over the bull. A wild bull was driven down a ramp; the girl ran towards it, grasped its horns, swung herself up and somersaulted onto the ground behind the animal just in time to catch the youth following after her. While the young couple carried out their first act of procreation in the palace, outside the blood flowed from the bull that had been sacrificed.

> The young people who consummated their sacred marriage after vaulting the bull came to know the nature of Eros... They knew existentially of the all-pervading power of Eros, and that the very life of nature is love, which is fraught with mortal danger but also accompanied by blessed fulfilment. One particular thing became impossible for them ever afterwards, and that was to misuse sex as a means of mere pleasure, to debase both Eros and

one's sexual partner to the level of mere object, something to have at one's disposal whenever one felt so inclined. Eros had overcome them once and for all with his superior force, which is one of the primal forces human beings encounter.[12]

Here we see how strongly sexual life was controlled by religion a long time before marriage became a Christian sacrament. Although it took place in a non-individualized realm, there was nothing arbitrary about it. People submitted to the rules given them by their rulers, for they knew that they had to learn self-control before allowing their instincts free rein.

Our age has different priorities. People seldom speak of self-control but rather of suppression and inhibitions. The advice given in former times, that to deny oneself something strengthens the will, has become unpopular. On the contrary, an 'enlightened' view invariably includes instruction in the use of contraceptives.

Primitive religions showed greater wisdom in the handling of the will than we do. They knew that the instincts involve elemental forces. In fact, they experienced these as actual beings, which one should approach only with caution and reverence. Their own knowledge of this was either instinctive or they were taught it by great leaders of humanity. Their own conscious thinking ability was very undeveloped.

As human consciousness slowly brightened and grew more awake, spirit and nature increasingly came to be regarded as opposite forces. This led to the tendency to think of natural attributes as inferior, and to suppress them; and this also applied to the realm of sex.

Ancient Judaism played a leading role here. Its historical task was to understand the spirit as distinct from nature in an age when most races or peoples still beheld the sense world as an outer garment of the gods. The Jewish God is invisible and does not permit himself to be portrayed as an image. Thus it is understandable that Judaism fought with real fury against the religious prostitution I referred to previously. It was a righteous battle, for human consciousness had changed and the time for this was past.

Yet marriage and sex life still maintained a strongly impersonal element in Jewish culture. Daughters were married off at their father's discretion and had to accommodate themselves to this. Copulation took place to guarantee the continuation of the tribe, and reproduction was its sole justification. This had deep significance, for this nation was creating the genealogy of the Messiah who was to be born among them. Actions of Old Testament women such as Thamar and Ruth can be understood solely in the light of the prophesied Messiah.[13] After becoming the widow of two sons of Judah, Thamar waylaid her father-in-law disguised as a whore so that despite her widowhood she might yet become a mother by a man of that tribe. The strategy proved successful. In a similar way Ruth offered herself to Boas, the nearest relative of her dead husband.

With a world-view of that kind it is clear that polygamy had its justification. As reproduction was considered to be the meaning and purpose of marriage and such tremendous significance was attached to it, a husband whose wife was sterile was in fact obliged to take a second wife.

In contrast to this, it is intrinsic to the principles of Christianity to consider human beings as individuals regardless of their racial, tribal or family ties. This outlook is incompatible with polygamy, and the Christian form of marriage is therefore monogamous from the outset.

Nevertheless it was a long time before people were really convinced that the most important aspect of all was an individual, unique relationship between two partners. The ascetic ideal in medieval times was that the only moral justification for a marital partnership was the production of offspring. Here, fundamentally, Christianity adopted the sexual ethics of Judaism.

Two hundred years ago a 'marriage of love' was still by no means the norm. Parents or other relatives arranged the marriages, which had, above all, to be within the same social class. There must always have been 'romantic love' and rebellion against parents' arrangements, as with Romeo and Juliet. In general, however, young people submitted, finding in their disposition of heart and mind, and in religious concepts, the strength to accept their destiny. There were by no means more unhappy marriages than there are today. People regarded marriage more as a practical arrangement. And if one's partner was affable and one was spared poverty and too much illness or death, there were grounds for satisfaction and for speaking of 'a fortunate marriage'.

During the German classical period, plays such as Schiller's *Love and Intrigue* caused a sensation because they rebelled against these conditions. It was only then that it really began to dawn on people that a loveless marriage was an unworthy state of affairs.

In orthodox Jewish circles, as is very beautifully and movingly portrayed in the musical *Fiddler on the Roof* by Joseph Stern, this change took place still later. Set at the beginning of the last century, it shows how the milkman Tewje, a paterfamilias and father of five daughters, is compelled to witness one daughter after the other wanting to marry 'for love'. This modern trend is difficult for the parents to understand, and in fact they wonder what love is; but eventually they have no choice but to accept.

Why did people all of a sudden feel that the basis for partnership had to be a soul relationship between two people, and that love belongs to marriage?

One reason for this was that human beings had grown beyond their former sense of being first and foremost part of a group. Family blood ties no longer upheld people as they had before, and they could therefore no longer see the sense in making this the sole vehicle for the continuation of a family or the increase of its wealth. There are a number of stories by Adalbert Stifter (1805–68) in which he endeavours to build a kind of bridge between the old and the new view. He describes parents doing the matchmaking for their children, yet without pressurizing them too much. Fate ordains that 'by chance' the young people concerned fall in love with one another. One of these stories is called 'The Pious Motto'[14]— the motto in question being that 'marriages are made in heaven'. While there may be no denying this, the story suggests, it's a good idea to give heaven a bit of help! Stifter combines warm-heartedness with sound common sense!

In cultural history we can trace how marriage came to be based on the power of attraction between two human beings and was idealized or romanticized in all sorts of ways, but that materialism was continually gaining ground at the same time. Thus by the end of the nineteenth century, although people strove for marriages based on love, the phenomenon of love was finally completely reduced to its physical and corporeal aspect.

Once again we find the conceptual basis for this coming

from Freud to whom love was basically a sexual phenomenon:

> On the basis of the fact that sexual (genital) love is the
> greatest source of human gratification and is actually the
> ideal of happiness we would suggest that all further grati-
> fication be sought in the realm of sexual relations and that
> genital eroticism be placed at the centre of life.[15]

Freud *thought* this, but a few decades' later people *lived* it, as
the last shreds of traditional morality were swept away. From
a certain point of view, therefore, we can say that it is our
present age that is witnessing the final exodus of human
beings from paradise, and that they have now become wholly
naked. The process of desanctifying nature is now complete,
and any further development in this direction can only lead
to perversion.

Christian Morgenstern (1871–1914), a contemporary of
Freud's, made a number of objections to this overemphasis
on sex. 'One might say that sex devours two thirds of all
spiritual potential,' he writes in his collection of aphorisms
entitled *Stufen* [Stages], and: 'I keep coming back to the fact
that our estimation of sexual love has reached pathological
dimensions today, and it is imperative we reverse the process.'

Precisely because life is increasingly based on externalities,
people nowadays have, however, become ever more aware
that this sort of apparently emancipated outlook encloses and
isolates their inner life egotistically within itself. Fundamentally they are looking for something quite different: love as an
endeavour to meet the other person and create a space for her
or him within their own being.

The Mystery of Love

What it (my love) really must mean to me is destiny,
and not merely the destiny I bring upon myself. I
must feel it as an inexorable inevitability, and not
merely in the morning and evening hours of
longing.

Christian Morgenstern

One of the wonders of history is that in the Middle Ages, alongside ecclesiastical religion, which actually governed all spiritual life, we see the blossoming of courtly love as a deepening and sublimation of eroticism. Men's longing for women was extolled not through sexual fulfilment but in poetic form. To begin with such love and devotion was self-evidently addressed to married women of the nobility. The lady is the mistress both of the knight's heart and of the castle. But as early as Walther von der Vogelweide we see the idea arising that the character and gentle disposition of women of lower birth was just as worthy of adoration as that of the gentry. Walther invented the word *frouwelin* ('little lady'), which does not mean 'Miss' as we use it today, but rather women of lower birth.

Darling little lady,
God bless you today and always!
If only I could express my desire better
I would be full glad.
What more can I say to you
—except nobody could love you more than I.

Alas! It gives me such pain.
People reproach me for serenading one of lowly birth.
Curse them for not understanding what real love is;
They have never experienced true love.
Those who love for the sake of wealth and beauty,
What kind of love is that?

This anticipated an attitude of mind that did not fully emerge until the Weimar classicists. The inherent mood reminds us of the love lyrics of the young Goethe.

In the centuries that followed, sex began to be intimately connected with the life of the soul. Love became entirely personal.

The specific mood that prevailed in the sacramental offering of sex in ancient times—that is, its impersonal quality—was now felt to be immoral, and in fact to belong to the realm of prostitution. I believe that even today, despite various other modern tendencies, many people—especially women—experience it this way. Simone de Beauvoir, who was consciously extremely free in her sexual relationships, said in an interview:

With me, sex has always been in conjunction with passionate love, so if I was prepared to have a relationship I would also feel sexual attraction. If I was not available I would not feel sexually excited.

Question: No sudden desires? No unpremeditated nights in which you found satisfaction with anybody, no matter whom?

Oh no, never! That is not my way at all. Maybe it is puritanical, or maybe it comes from my education. Be this as it may, it has never happened. Not even when I had nothing on the go and was without sex for a while. I would never have dreamt of looking for some man . . .[16]

Simone de Beauvoir was a modern and emancipated woman. She did not say in the interview that she refuses occasional romances, but only that she cannot imagine a physical relationship without inner, emotional participation.

Her life is yet another startling example of the fact that monogamy is the only possible option for strong individuals. Her union with Jean-Paul Sartre, without marriage ties or a shared home or any vows, was nevertheless so strong and absolute that they could grant one another complete freedom, in the conviction that this could not violate the fact that they so clearly belonged together.

In the natural world of animal coupling, male and female are attracted to one another purely sexually, without any soul quality. If people base a physical relationship on a loving, emotional connection, they ascend to the human level where they are not attracted 'as a given' but where, in addition, two destinies seek one another. The ability to regard destiny as something brought upon us by inner soul experience and not by outer circumstances indicates a stage of evolution that humanity has only attained in recent centuries. This inner awareness can actually be distinguished from spontaneous feelings of love by a knowledge that *this person is my destiny. I know he belongs to me, even if for a time I love someone else more than he.* We can call this feeling the 'destiny instinct' for it comes from within, from the same depths of soul as the life of instinct. This feeling is not always so unambiguous as it is with Simone de Beauvoir. Experience also shows that it can be weakened by a multiplicity of sexual relationships, as physical closeness and intimacy can easily cause mistakes and illusions. This can produce great uncertainty: *Who really belongs to me?* Rushing rapidly into intimate relationships does not help us to get to know one another really well, and can actually hinder this.

Not every connection between people of the opposite gender needs to have something to do with sex. In the course of the evolution of humanity, people's soul life has become more fluid and free. This has brought with it the possibility of ensouling sex, and a diverse range of experience in the erotic sphere. Eros and Sexus belong to altogether different worlds.

Ever since the classical age, literature has portrayed an innumerable variety of love stories in which inner qualities of soul are described with ever-greater subtlety. We can speak of a 'sublimation' that may often even be increased by a (perhaps enforced) renunciation of sexual relations. This prompts all Goethe's love lyrics. People often find fault with him for having so many erotic relationships. In actual fact he was constantly forced to exercise restraint: think for instance of his love for Lotte Buff, who was engaged, and Charlotte von Stein who was married.

The Romantic period yielded the wonderfully delicate and deep relationship between Novalis and his fiancée Sophie, who died at the age of 15. What he learned from his relationship first to a child and then to a departed soul affected and transfigured not only all his poetry but also his erotic imagination.

Let us also remember Adalbert Stifter who was never able to marry the girl he loved, and who, alongside his respectable marriage, which left him unfulfilled, had a constant dream of eventual fulfilment. This enabled him to write the novella *Brigitte* that is such a beautiful and mature description of love between older people who, knowing one another from their youth but being separated by destiny, have a mutually fruitful union in old age without the distraction of sex. A similar picture with a magic of its own is described in his novel *Der Nachsommer* [Indian Summer] 1857.

We could continue with examples of this sort right up to our own time. The theme of forgoing love often takes the form of an abundant sex life bringing repeated disappointments until restraint is practised for the sake of experiencing the whole range of emotions. I am thinking here for instance of the very sensitive short story by Katherine Mansfield (1888–1923), entitled 'Psychology'.[17] She describes two friends, a man and a woman, meeting over a cup of tea and enthusiastically discussing literature. They get on so well together that they can be completely open and honest with one another.

> And the best of it was they were both of them old enough to enjoy their adventure to the full without any stupid emotional complication. Passion would have ruined everything; they quite saw that. Besides, all that sort of thing was over and done with for both of them—he was thirty-one, she was thirty—they had had their experiences, and very rich and varied they had been, but now was the time for harvest.

But silence suddenly descends upon them, one full to the brim with inexpressible, hidden things.

> They faltered, wavered, broke down, were silent. Again they were conscious of the boundless, questioning dark. Again, there they were—two hunters, bending over their fire, but hearing suddenly from the jungle beyond a shake of wind and a loud, questioning cry...

They know that their precious friendship is in danger. They do not want merely to yield to it and see what happens. So they cease abruptly and part. Is it all over? At first sight it appears so. The story is very open-ended, yet it is made clear that the love that has not been expressed rises to a new level and is transformed.

Often we are very awkward and lacking in subtlety when it comes to noticing delicate soul processes. We really should not fail to acknowledge and appreciate the conquests of literature in this realm since the classical age, dismissing them as merely 'romantic', but should regard them instead as steps towards liberation from the life of instinct. 'It is time for the harvest'.

Surely it's time
for immemorial pains to bear fruit? Can't we finally
lovingly free ourselves from our lover, pass quivering on?
As the arrow surpasses the string, gathers force to become
more than itself as it flies—for where can we rest?

This was the question Rilke asked in his Duino Elegies. He speaks, too, of

how much more loving
seem the abandoned ones than those
whose desire is quenched.

Love needs to be learned in solitude. Only on our own can we concentrate our soul forces and render them strong enough for the greatest service of love.

But as for the people who have already thrown themselves together and can no longer define nor distinguish them-selves, to the extent that they no longer possess anything that is really themselves, how are they to find a way out of their isolation when they have already thrown solitude away? They act out of mutual helplessness. And if, with the best will in the world, they avoid convention (such as marriage) they fall into the clutches of just as lethal a conventional solution: for them everything in their whole milieu is nothing but a kind of—convention. For if people act out of a partnership they have rushed into and that is not what one could call conscious, every action is conventional. Every relationship arising out of this sort of confusion has its conventional pattern, however unusual it is (i.e., immoral in the normal sense); even separation would in fact be a conventional step to take, an impersonal, chance decision lacking in strength and leading nowhere.[18]

We need distance to perceive what destiny wants of us. Life has become complex. Threads of destiny bind us together in manifold ways. The separation of a couple enhances their consciousness only if it is experienced as a loss, but not if one erases the other from consciousness. The test of *what* one actually misses after separation can tell a lot about the nature of a friendship.

A real problem that often occurs is that an attraction at a soul level is misunderstood and pushed down too rapidly into the physical realm. Multiplicity is justified in the soul realm, but if people imagine they have to express all their friendships physically, something has slipped down too far. This makes any permanent connection impossible and can lead to regrettable human tragedies such as we saw in the biography of Franziska von Reventlow, mentioned at the outset.

It is a tendency of our times either to rush very rapidly into sexual contact or to maintain a relationship on a completely impersonal, businesslike level. This points to a certain lack of

imagination. We have by no means exhausted all the possibilities which lie between these two extremes.

There are so many opportunities for togetherness in which
relationships flourish at a soul level, including with people of
the opposite sex. These can enrich life tremendously. After
all, we are first and foremost human beings and only secondly
male or female.

Looking for one relationship after another in the hope that
the next one will be less disappointing may be connected
with one of the problems of our time—a kind of dilution of
feeling. This is probably caused by the fact that it would be
unendurable to accompany with feelings all the information
and impressions we are inundated with. People protect
themselves by shutting off. As a result, weakness of feeling has
become a disease of the age. Goethe was still able to enjoy the
happiness of love utterly and completely. But equally, he felt
the pains of love just as intensely. Nowadays we are scarcely
able to experience such deep sorrow as that of Goethe's
young Werther.

We no longer have much aptitude for 'romantic' love, but
we have acquired a new faculty: an inner distance from
ourselves, so that we can as it were look upon our feelings
from above. If this is consciously practised people can make
progress in their feeling relationships.

This also involves observing and accepting the fact that the
way women feel has a different quality from the way men
feel. A woman's feeling life is doubtless more inwardly differentiated than a man's, and women therefore sometimes
find this a cause of disappointment. On the other hand, it can
be unbearable if a woman's feelings work alone in enclosed
isolation. Some women novelists portray every single nuance
of the happy, tormented or disappointed feelings of the

woman in love, without describing even the merest outward circumstances of the man she loves.

The most beautiful descriptions of a woman's inner life still come from men. This is probably due to the fact that their outwardly directed mode of perception—a woman's inner life also being external to them—enables them to give clearer descriptions than a woman, who may have great sensitivity in her feelings but is more caught up in herself.

A woman tends to exalt a feeling relationship and to love, in reality, an ideal image of her own creation that is only partly like the actual man. If she loves intensely she can be under tremendous illusions. She loves an ideal but she cannot connect it with reality.

In his Alcestis, Thornton Wilder (1897–1975) presents a subtle and accurate picture of a woman's nature.[19] Alcestis cannot initially respond to the great love of the young King Admetus—a love that is clearly destined—because she loves the god Apollo more than him. To be a priestess of the god in Delphi would fulfil her highest aspirations. But he does not appoint her. She is in total confusion when a seer informs her that the god Apollo has come among mortals as a swineherd. Which swineherd is he? It gradually dawns on her that the god has distributed himself among all human beings, entering into them so that there is now a divine element concealed in everyone—which means also in King Admetus. Now that she recognizes the divine essence in the sensory world, she becomes capable of a rich and fulfilled marriage.

When a woman is in love everything becomes unimportant apart from the object of her love. Since it is so focused, her love can also become narrow. However intensely a man loves he will not so easily forget his other duties. More outwardly orientated, he identifies himself with

his actions and achievements. Research has found that men
suffer much more from being unemployed than women do,
experiencing the lack of achievement as wounding to their
self-esteem. A woman is more inwardly focused, is more self-
contained, and can therefore cope with such a situation more
easily.

From this perspective, therefore, we ought not to view it as
altogether unjust that, generally speaking, men are not
expected to give up their profession for the sake of love. As
this is something that necessarily more often involves
women, it seems initially that love is a harder destiny for
women than men. This is true in so far as they have fewer
opportunities for manoeuvre. However, if their love is deep
and sincere, both partners will feel the working of destiny.
Having chosen the path of love, it becomes apparent that
something beyond ordinary human understanding inter-
venes: either the path descends below the human level into a
self-centred satisfying of instinct or ascends above it into
inevitabilities of destiny from which there is no turning back.
Rilke expresses this in his poem 'Eros':

Masks, bring masks to dazzle Eros
for who can bear his radiant face
when like the grandeur of the summer solstice
he makes spring's prelude suddenly gather pace?

Abruptly, amidst easy chatter
all changes and grows serious ... a cry ...
And over them he casts the nameless shiver
of an inner sanctum, soundlessly.

Lost, so suddenly, O lost!
Swiftly beings divine embrace.

Destiny is born and life recast:
a spring weeps in the inwardness.

Destiny, which can eventually assume form in the child they
have together, calls on the husband to centre and focus his
outwardly directed energies, and on the wife to expand her
focused soul forces over a wider realm. Thus, in a successful
partnership, polar opposite forces can be harmonized.

The Mystery of Love

Delicate, subtle play takes on fixed form.
The path we tread grows ever narrower.
Enchantment that enlarged us, made us freer
Soon rules over us like day and night.
Often alarmed by all too certain joy
We wish ourselves again in love's first germ
Of tenderness, from which pure joys arose.
In vain! The cry of something coming into being
Has sounded, and the breath of heaven we felt
Breeds bitterness, just sharpens our desire.
Often we find we're driven apart, cannot
Distinguish between hate or love:
We have to hurt each other with painful words,
To plumb the deeper truth of life.
Songs whisper to us of a mysterious warning:
Whoever seeks for ecstasy reaps death.
Yet this grave message holds no more alarm
To us tied through long ages to the dangers
Of the blood. Death, we lovers know you well.
We see the star that circles in you and rests!
Yet when we flow together and unite,
Already seem to touch the lovely star,

It fades to nothing, bearing pleasure hence.
And we cover our faces and grieve.
Beloved, come,
Let us dare greater things; let's shake
The world to pieces, full of death's joy!
Let's break the last bridge of our longing, emerge
From slumber into riper birth, awaken
In life's highest dream. And then
No room for casual procreation.
Eternity has sounded, the eggshell shatters:
The way to a new shore lies free before us.
Deeds need to be done, in which we grow
Maturer, emancipate ourselves from dull
Promptings of our sex. O most loving woman
In building the archetypal temple, we
Shall gloriously build ourselves.
The door of growth is open wide.
Eros now begins to be embodied.
Deep, resonant circles interpenetrate;
Abundant life seeks to proliferate,
Seeks to die free into the beloved
And resurrect there to a whole new state.

Hans Carossa (1878–1956)

What Makes a Relationship Last?

Things that belong together must conjoin;
That understand each other, the other find.
What is good, together bind,
What loves, entwine.
What obstructs must soften,
What crooked, be smoothed and evened,
What's distant meet and mend,
What sprouts grow grain.

Give me faithfully your hand:
Be my brother and never turn
Your gaze from me until your end.
One temple—where we kneel
One goal—to which we long
One good—to which we sail
One heaven—our single song.

Novalis

The contradictory element in a love affair is that the peaks of real fulfilment are so short and transient, and yet we would like them to be a basis for a permanent attachment. Why is this? Is Rilke right when he says the following about people in love?

I know
that your touch is pure joy because your caresses
contain you, because the place your touch
tenderly hides does not vanish, because
beneath it you feel the enduring pulse—almost
an eternity of embrace.

Most people are of course so blasé today that they no longer talk overmuch about the 'eternal' nature of love. Our attitude is such that our sense of reality is based chiefly on what is conveyed by our senses; we therefore expect permanence to lie in this same sphere. Thus a physical, i.e. sexual relationship, unless it is merely a fling and is intended as such, invariably has something about it that gives the initial pull to remain with one another and live together. Perhaps this is even more the case today because our ability to stay together is decreasing all the time.

When two people decide to live together, the relationship between them is no longer a private affair but now becomes part of the social sphere. No longer alone, they require a space to live, and wish their partnership to be respected by others—which means that a kind of 'social substance' has been created, whether their partnership has the legal form of a marriage or not.

When friends and acquaintances comment on the partnership, this is perfectly justified and not mere prying. The relationship one forms with another person is different depending on whether that person is 'single' or is someone else's partner. It becomes different again if the two separate. You may be friendlier with one person than the other. In this case, should you no longer associate with the other? Problems of this kind can arise.

We have already touched on the fact that the Church determined social structures in the Middle Ages. It demanded marital fidelity since marriage was regarded as a sacrament and was therefore insoluble. In her book *Geschlecht und Kultur* [Sex and Culture], Rosa Mayreder (1858–1938) says that the medieval Church regarded asceticism as the highest human ideal, and this was evident from the vows taken by the monks. This had the following effect on the institution of marriage:[20]

Asceticism in its absolute form was not a general requirement. Within its set limits, however, the stipulated form of monogamous marriage was no less inexorable than absolute asceticism. Any departure from the vows of inviolable fidelity in marriage was just as disgraceful and sinful as a departure from the monastic vow of inviolable abstention. The absolute restriction of sexual intercourse to married couples, regardless of any other considerations, is a fundamental law of the ascetic view of Christian marriage.

People did not always adhere to this, of course. Medieval history is full of adultery. Nevertheless the principle held good that fidelity was supposed to belong to marriage, and any deviation from this principle was always considered a disgrace.

People are justified nowadays in resisting any kind of external moral pressure. Traditional social structures have fallen away. We should therefore consider this as the norm, and not complain about the failure of so many marriages. If people succeed, nevertheless, in upholding a strong partnership, we look on it as a real personal achievement.

Nowadays it has become quite common to live together as man and wife without getting married. This state of affairs has, however, only recently come about. Even 40 years ago it would not have worked, simply because such a couple would not have found anywhere to live—not to mention the fact that a self-respecting girl would often refuse to be just someone's 'mistress'.

Nowadays nobody is *bound* to get married. Even pregnancy is in itself no cogent reason any more. Life is not easy for a single mother, but she and her child are not a social disgrace as used to be the case.

This development can only be welcomed. We cannot speak of individual freedom as long as people are forced to follow prescribed patterns, whether for legal, economic, social or moral reasons.

Under these circumstances are there any reasons for still staying together when difficulties occur? In other words, is marital fidelity still a relevant virtue?

Dr Ruth Westheimer, an American counsellor and writer on sex, said the following in an interview:

> In today's society it is not so easy to maintain an absolutely dependable and loyal relationship for a whole lifetime. When it works it is wonderful, and from my heart I would wish everybody such a partnership. It would be wrong to prescribe absolute fidelity. In one's own life one can set oneself the goal of an absolutely faithful partnership, but you cannot make this ideal into a principle for everyone else to follow. Besides, this would be a totally unrealistic demand.

Her next comment is all the more interesting as it comes not from a moral principle but simply from sound common sense:

> Most people, whether they are younger or older, want just one life partner. I find it hard to believe that anyone would intrinsically want a number of partnerships simultaneously or in quick succession.

This is a remarkable statement. When theologians felt incapable of believing in life after death any longer, medical sources, drawn from a large volume of case reports, simul-taneously revealed that patients believed there must be such a thing. Similarly, when the Church can no longer demand fidelity, sexual theorists discover that most people do not actually want several partners—not now for moral reasons, but out of their own natural feeling.

That polygamy is an almost unbearable way of life for modern people is described very movingly in a little book by Miriama Bâ, an African woman from Senegal, entitled 'Such a long letter',[21] and published in Germany only a few years ago. Bâ had the same material standard of living as we do (car, fridge, etc.). She and her male friend were students. They fell in love and were married as soon as possible. They built a house and had a large family. Later on the husband fell in love with a friend of their daughter's, and as the Senegalese are Mohammedans nothing prevented him from marrying her as well. He purchased another house into which he moved with his young wife. This is perfectly legitimate there. A divorce is not necessary; on the contrary many husbands ring the changes at night among their many wives. This did not happen in this case. His first wife, deeply hurt, would not have accepted him.

> Just think that I loved this man passionately, gave him 30 years of my life, and bore him 12 children. It was not enough for him to bring a rival into my life. In loving another he at the same time erased his past both morally and physically.

African women accepted polygamy for hundreds of years. Why will they no longer do so?

Because women there, too, have awakened to the individual ego and see marriage as a relationship of one ego to another. So infidelity makes them feel betrayed in their innermost being.

Fidelity is not a feeling but a responsible relationship of ego to ego. Despite this there is a strong tendency nowadays to make promiscuity an acceptable way of life. It is often considered normal for people who are geographically separated for a while to choose another partner, at least temporarily. Physical proximity is thought absolutely essential for maintaining a relationship. This very regrettable trend arises out of a one-sidedly materialistic idea of love.

A sexual relationship is obviously not possible in the absence of one's partner—therefore one cannot 'enjoy' oneself. On the other hand this is a wonderful opportunity to strengthen and deepen a soul relationship. This will be a missed opportunity if one looks for a temporary 'replacement'. By doing so we deprive ourselves of a maturation process that involves putting ourselves to the test to see whether we actually only want something for ourselves from the relationship or feel real love, i.e. unselfish interest in the other individual.

It is obviously unrealistic to demand fidelity of another. Yet when we give our love we naturally expect love in return. Can we have confidence in another person—and this word is linguistically related to fidelity—if we cannot depend on him or her to be faithful? In such a case, surely, this means we cannot avoid harbouring a certain mistrust, and this sort of situation makes many people feel very insecure.

Underlying this state of affairs is a misconception of freedom, which confuses it with liberty. People want to leave every avenue open and avoid any real decisions, because these tie them. They do not want to take the consequences of their own actions. It is hard to cope with the freedom to make decisions. When we have this freedom we become aware how weak and insecure we are. Someone forced to do something can complain about the person who exerts pressure on him. The responsibility for our own decisions, on the other hand, falls upon us. A fair amount of ego strength is required to cope with this. Everyone wants to be free today, but few people know how to set about it. The same thing applies to women's liberation.

Scarcely anyone has engaged with the concept of freedom so precisely and consistently as Rudolf Steiner in *The Philosophy of Freedom*. According to him an action is free only if its motive is grasped inwardly and independently, and not if it is determined in any way from without, even by conforming to generally accepted moral principles:

> The actions of people who only act because they accept certain moral rules are the result of those principles, which happen to be contained in their moral code. They are superior automatons who carry out orders. If a stimulus is injected into their minds the clockwork of their moral principles will set itself in motion and run the course described for initiating actions deemed Christian, or humane, or unselfish, or intended to promote cultural progress... Human beings are free only to the extent that they are able, at any moment of their lives, to be their own guide; a moral deed is my own deed only if it can be called free in this sense.

The fundamental idea in Rudolf Steiner's book, although written over a hundred years ago, has in no way become less topical, but possibly even more so. He calls the source of a modern person's self-determined motives 'moral intuition'. This presumes one has the insight necessary to see the objective context on which a deed will impact.

That he in no way means doing whatever one pleases can

be seen from a letter he wrote 30 years later (1913) in answer to the question of whether marriage was in a state of crisis. He began by saying that in a marriage a couple place themselves into a social complex in the widest sense. Then he continues:

> This makes any discussion of the principle of marriage impossible if it is viewed solely from the point of view of the personal interests of the couple about to be married. The social aspect will have to be taken into account in so far as marriage, which by its very nature contributes so much to the preservation of the social fabric, can be regarded as a *stable* relationship that can be relied on once it comes about. Individual interests may well conflict with more general ones; the solution to the problem must then surely be that individuals do not set their own interests above those of their social environment.

Then he goes on to say that as soon as children are involved, the question of marriage becomes a family question:

> Anyone who can rightly estimate the potential inherent in this relationship ... both now and into the far future, will realize that in so far as both the husband and the wife should be equally attached to a child of theirs, this is a bond that works back on the stability of the marriage and doubtless requires it. However, I cannot see that the modern principle of marriage contains anything other than the question of greater or lesser solidarity and insolubility of the bond. All the other questions boil down to this, even if people are not conscious of it in every case. As soon as marriage is placed in its essential setting we see that both the social and the family aspect always force us to acknowledge its stability whatever the balance between

personal and other interests may be. In things of this kind people cannot create institutions to suit individual needs, but have to adapt them to what exists overall.

According to Rudolf Steiner, life can of course bring about a certain opposition between the overall social context and our own personal experience.

What follows from this for many marriages does not at all depend on the nature of the marriage but on things beyond its scope. For instance marriages can become unhappy even though the misfortune does not stem from the marriage at all but from the fact that one or both of the marriage partners were not brought up to be compatible or tolerant. This directs our attention away from an individual institution to the major contemporary problems of education and upbringing. And as long as these are in the melting pot to the extent they are today, citing a single instance does not get us very far. A view of the world and of life which gives a person inner peace and harmony will also have its effect on marriage—one that will not be disturbed by the marriage form.[22]

It comes as an initial surprise that Steiner's argument touches neither on the field of psychology nor morals. The reasons that speak for a lasting marriage are sought entirely in the outer world, in the way the couple become part of human society and how they keep their family together or provide the best possible care for their children.

For many people with marriage problems today, this last point is a very acute and often painful experience. Children of a divorce always carry a great burden with them which can certainly be mitigated by reasonable arrangements but can

never be avoided altogether. The destiny invoked by a sexual
relationship assumes form in the children; it cannot be
revoked and it calls for permanence.

In an article on sex written from a purely biological
viewpoint, Professor Friedrich Schaller speaks of a child's
'natural claim' to two parents.[23] He emphasizes that he does
not mean a 'right' but a natural claim. He draws the conclusion that 'People who consider marriage to be solely the
private affair of two sexual partners mistake both its biological
and its ethical character.' This is strikingly similar to Rudolf
Steiner's conception of marriage as a social institution.

The negative aspect of a love match is that it hugely
increases the expectations invested in a marriage. In this
matter-of-fact age should we not be able to consider human
partnership, however much love it draws on, in a more
matter-of-fact way? A great many difficulties arise, surely,
from excess of feeling, simply because the demands we make
on our partner are too great. He ought to help us, make us
happy, etc. Might we not be happier without such expectations? Marriage as an institution is not to blame for bringing
such frequent disappointment. Married bliss is a gift of special
moments, while life partnership is daily reality, involving
inner and outer work. Sharing the same feelings is not the
same thing as living together.

In every partnership there arises over time an almost tangible web of things shared, of life substance. If a long-
standing marriage breaks up, and only one of the partners
desires this, the other one frequently feels the separation as
the sundering of something that has grown together—like
killing something living. On the whole, women have more
of a feeling than men do of the presence and cultivation of
these imponderables. Creating the atmosphere in a home is

very often the wife's business, since very few men are capable of this in the same way. They are however certainly able to perceive and appreciate this atmosphere. In this realm the wife is most often the giver and the husband the recipient.

The fact that intimate togetherness of two human beings gives rise not only to atmosphere at a soul level but also physical life is one of the greatest wonders of life, and opens the way to the social sphere. Together a couple learn to make way for a third, and discover in their child features of both partners and also something completely new. The child is both a confirmation of their togetherness and a reaching beyond it, and urges their shared responsibility. If, however, divisive behaviour becomes a habit between two parents, bringing the sort of difficulties that can become obsessive, then the child can seem like a living reproach.

In his 'Children's Story'[24] Peter Handke introduces a scene in which, as a husband, wife and child on a car journey take a break on the slope of a hill, the sort of imponderables that have grown between them run their usual course:

A quarrel starts between the husband and wife, similar to many they have had before and probably—the husband thought yet again—in exactly the same words as those exchanged in similar moments by discordant couples the world over.

(So far he hadn't wished to have a final separation, because an official third person, however experienced and competent he might be, could not possibly know the ins and outs of the three of them, and any judicial ruling would have struck him as presumptuous). Yet at the same time the quarrel gets serious and, without realizing it, and as though violating the peace of the countryside, he falls back into the dreary and monotonous round of their compulsive mutual reproaches.

When he finally looks up he sees that the child has gone off by himself to sit down a long way from the two grown-ups. In the distance his face looks pale and grim. Bilberries are gleaming in the sun all over the hillside. At the foot of the hill there is a lake. It is a very bright day interspersed with the heavy shadows of clouds. The three figures squat there like white monuments.

This captures something of the mood of the hopelessness and tragedy of human discord where a third person—a child in this case—is also involved.

But parents also constantly experience the very real uniting quality of obligations implicit in the presence of a child, on an outing, for instance, if they accidentally go the wrong way. If the couple were on their own, in their thoroughly exhausted state, they might begin to blame one another. But they have the child with them who has to walk much further on his small legs or be carried, so they pull themselves together and keep the child happy.

Children who remain children forever—that is children with disabilities—or an invalid or grandmother who needs looking after can be a tremendously uniting element in a family. Otherwise perhaps, each person might go their own way, but since someone has to be on-call all the time they have to work together and share a rota; and they may wake up suddenly to the fact that though the partnership has burdens to bear, it is more harmonious and intimate than it was before.

Disasters such as war, floods or illness can have a similar effect, because they distract people from their own psycho-logical problems. Remarkable things can happen in this respect. A young wife who was expecting a baby had an abortion because her marriage was going so badly that she thought a separation was imminent. Shortly afterwards she developed cancer, and throughout her years of pain, until her death, she could not have had a more devoted nurse than her husband. Another wife broke away from a marriage that she found unbearable, and had affairs with many other men until she contracted AIDS. After that she lived with her husband again, who surrounded her with care and created new forms of tenderness, so that she was happier than she ever dreamed she could be.

Catastrophes and accidents can mean that people disengage from the superficialities of everyday life with which they frequently torment themselves and others, and direct their attention to essentials. In this way, sometimes, the true being of the person one has committed one's life to surfaces in a quite new way.

Couldn't we achieve this without catastrophe? This question seems to me to point towards something extraordinarily important. In every marriage, common interests should exist as a third element on which the couple can focus their attention and work. By doing so they participate in a process that involves them both. Children grow up. To ensure that the relationship does not stagnate and become merely habitual, they need 'spiritual children'. It is helpful for many couples to have the same profession, in which they collaborate. Others consider it of special importance for each of them to have their particular field of interest in which they are more competent than the other, realizing how enriching it is to discuss and share experiences. We can be particularly thankful at the realization that something has succeeded which would have been impossible without our spouse.

There is a kind of process of fertilization at an inner level, too, just as there is in the sexual sphere, although here the roles are not so clearly assigned. Often a wife will stimulate and 'fertilize' her husband, but it also happens the other way round. 'Spiritual children' produced between a man and his wife are more common than one imagines, and they rank among the most beautiful results of human cohabitation.

There are ever fewer people who have first-hand experience of a long-lasting life partnership. The tangible sense that partners' destinies can fuse together is one of the most important experiences. There is more to this than the outward aspect of living together in the same place, knowing the same people, going on holiday together, and gradually having more and more experiences in common. It can also happen, for instance, that for outer or inner reasons one of them proves unable to accomplish some of their life's tasks. The other can then give support and encouragement, or even take on the task instead. This—taking on someone else's destiny—is one of the greatest, most Christian opportunities life has to offer, and by no means restricted to the partnership of marriage.

For example, certain ideas and social impulses may be ripe for realization, yet the one whose task this rightfully is may be unable to act on them. In such a case, someone else who perceives the needs and circumstances can renounce developing their own abilities and potential, and take on the destined task of the other. We should not worry that this will detract from their own self-realization or destiny. In fact it is interesting to observe that events belonging solely to the destiny of one spouse or partner of a couple can occur precisely when the other is absent. We usually only notice the wise guidance governing such things when we cast our minds back years later.

The Mythical Roots of Motherliness

In solitude are throned the goddesses,
No place surrounds them. Time still less;
Only to speak of them disconcerts us.
They are the Mothers!
    Mothers!
        Do you feel dread?
The Mothers! Mothers!—Strangely it resonates.
Wondrous also: goddesses, unknown
To mortals, not gladly named by us.
Delve in the deepest depths to reach their dwelling;
That we have need of them is your own fault.

J. W. von Goethe

The demythologizing of our lives has swept away many an old superstition.

It has, however, also led to the desecration and trivialization of realms of life people used to approach only with the greatest respect and awe. Sex, pregnancy and birth have been reduced to the purely medical facts involved. What a mother-to-be has to put up with from doctors and clinics is frequently undignified and humiliating, and breeds insecurity in a realm that intrinsically belongs to the essence of womanhood.[25]

The religious aspect of motherhood that still existed in earlier ages can give every woman the strength to accept, with gratitude and respect, her body's potential as a source of life.

Goethe's 'Faust' has to descend to the 'Mothers' in order to make the archetype of the beautiful Helen appear in the earthly world. The words introducing this chapter are Mephisto's answer to Faust's urgent question.

The archetype of motherhood is not something relegated to the past. It is buried—deeply maybe—in everyone's psyche, but present all the same. Fairy tales speak of it. And telling children such stories is real nourishment for the soul and more 'enlightening' than the highly regarded, premature anatomy lessons, from which neither children nor adults can really learn about the source of life.

That babies 'grow in Mummy's tummy' is only a very limited aspect of the matter, of course. In actual fact a mother has the task of accompanying and escorting souls, and a great deal depends on her knowing this.

In former times, the descent of a child's soul was often seen in the image of a bird. The stork is the best-known bringer of children. Images such as this were not an avoidance of reality but a presentation of it at a higher level. Small children still sense this today. For instance, a child who had been 'enlightened' on many occasions still put a lump of sugar on the window sill for the stork. He was once again told the facts of life, but without success. When the child's mother tried for the third time, he interrupted her angrily with the words 'You're lying!'[26]

How can children, who make nothing of ideas such as 'sexual attraction' or 'eroticism', understand the parents' role in incarnation? Only images can convey a comprehensive meaning in simple form.

A six-year-old child with three younger siblings was given all the usual information, including being allowed to feel the unborn child moving inside his mother's body. Yet one day he exclaimed: 'My mother and father wanted to eat a peach

one day, and when they cut it open to share it I crawled out.'
This story, from a Japanese book of stories, seemed more
intelligible to the child than all the other explanations.[27]

In many regions folk traditions tell of babies coming out of
the water: the baby stream in the Alps, the nursery well in
Alsace or 'Mother Holle's Pond' in Hessen. Water is an
image of life. Mother Holle (whose name means 'the gracious
one') was originally a fertility goddess. In the well-known
Grimm's fairy tale of that name, the girl driven out by her
stepmother finds her true mother in Mother Holle. The way
to get to her is down the well, in other words through the
water realm. Spatial conceptions that belong to the earthly
world lose their significance there. When the girl plunges
into the well she arrives in an underworld. Oddly enough,
this is also *above* the human world, for when she shakes out
the bedclothes at Mother Holle's it snows down on earth. As
the source of life and of motherliness Mother Holle's king-
dom is both below and above the everyday world. To reach
this strange realm is frightening at first, and so the girl is
initially afraid of Mother Holle, although the latter is good to
her.

Here we have a reference, in childlike form, to a world of
which Goethe speaks when his Faust goes to the 'Mothers'
(Goethe's source being Plutarch). 'What is the path like?'
Faust asks, and Mephisto describes it thus:

Descend then! I could also say: Ascend!
'Tis all the same. Escape from the created
to shapeless forms in liberated spaces!

Faust shudders when he hears the word 'Mothers'. He knows
one has to forsake the spatial world in order to reach them. It is
the same fear as that mentioned in the story of Mother Holle.

In the legend, Mother Holle is often described as young
and beautiful. She sits beside lakes and wells and combs her
long golden hair. Sometimes she is also presented as terrible
and frightening. She accompanies the army of the wild
huntsman (Odin), which is on the move during the Twelve
Holy Nights between Christmas and Epiphany. There is
another legend which describes her on the night of All Souls
as the 'Mother of the Dead', accompanying the procession of
children who have died.

In these diverse images this mythical 'great mother' appears
in threefold form: she is the beautiful young goddess of birth
(white); the mature goddess of fertility and nutrition connected with the full moon (red); and the terrifying goddess of
death (black). The threefold goddess thus encompasses all
aspects of life from birth to death.[28]

In its archetypal sense, 'mother' is what one turns to in
order to find protection and help when everything else fails.
Not only children, but sick or dying people often turn
towards her. In fairy tales she sometimes even gives help from
beyond the threshold of death, i.e. in the story of the Juniper
Tree or Cinderella. Each day Cinderella finds renewed
strength by praying at her mother's grave, and her 'fairy
godmother' gives her the royal garments that help her to
unite with the king's son.

There is a real difference between being the mother of a
daughter or of a son. Demeter and Persephone are a mythical
image of the mother-daughter relationship. Demeter's
lament over the theft of her daughter makes the whole world
infertile, and without her Persephone would have remained
forever in the underworld. Whereas the feminine qualities of
a mother come to fulfilment in her daughter, she strives to
'become a man in her son', as Morgenstern puts it. We have

an archetype of this in the Egyptian goddess Isis who, after her husband Osiris is murdered, conceives his son Horus through a ray of light from the world of the dead. She enables her feminine primacy to be succeeded by a masculine sovereignty—a theme we will return to later.

The mother image also contains its opposite: a stepmother, who is not necessarily the father's second wife. The child's own mother can equally be a 'non-mother', which is often the case in the original versions of some fairy tales, such as 'Snow White' for instance. Being a mother requires the development of quite specific qualities, such as devotion, patience, sacrifice, perseverance, renunciation, care, etc. When a woman's egotism and self-centredness are so great that they predominate over all these other qualities, she cannot become a mother. We all, surely, have something of the stepmother in us.

This can take various directions. The mother of Hansel and Gretel would prefer to eat her bread herself than share it. She is heartless, cold and calculating. In the earthly material sense, when bread is short it is definitely more advantageous to have two mouths to feed rather than four. But would any real mother keep food for herself and let her children starve? Fairy tales never tire of telling us that a compassionate and loving heart is subject to different laws than those of calculating reason. There are numerous examples of scenes such as that of the poor girl who arrives among the three little men in the wood and shares her dry bread with them. The little men then show her where strawberries are growing in the middle of winter. Her stepsister takes the same path but does not share her bread, and gets nothing.

Snow White's mother has a different motive for wanting to get rid of her daughter. As the girl's beauty increases, the mother feels she is put in the shade, and jealousy leaves her no peace. Women who become mothers very young and are still in the bloom of youth themselves can easily be jealous of a growing daughter. There are instances like the slim and well-groomed woman of 35 who looked ten years younger, and whose main interest in life was her male conquests. This made her a veritable stepmother to her sensitive and inti-midated 15-year-old daughter. The mother was embarrassed to have such a grown-up daughter and could not bear her presence at home. The child had to grow up between boarding school and her grandparents.[29] This is not to say that one cannot understand the attitude of a young woman who obviously became a mother before she found herself. It is only that she could not be a real mother to her child under those circumstances.

In both these cases, stepmotherhood consists of too strong an element of repudiation. But the reverse can be the case. A mother so totally consumed by her motherliness that she cannot break away from it at all also becomes a stepmother. She does not want to accept that small children get bigger. Motherhood also involves letting children go. A play by Ernst Barlach (1870–1938), 'The Dead Day',[30] portrays the sort of mother who says to her son: 'I have devoted my life to you. If you leave me my life will be over!' She robs her son of his future because she wants everything to stay as it is.

In fairy tales we have the image of the witch who entices children to her and tries to eat them. She is the anti-mother who, instead of allowing the child to emerge from her body into the world, tries to consume him again. Other stories tell of her turning a young person 'to stone', so that he will remain as he is and cannot leave her or, in other words, make any developmental progress.

Every mother can benefit from asking herself which of the stepmotherly characteristics she most tends towards: whether she is calculating (the time I spend on my child and my family I could spend on my own self-realization) or envious (my daughter is young and I am growing old) or selfish (my child should remain with me and make me happy).

Being a mother surely always means being present when one is needed and stepping back when one is not. This is certainly asking a great deal. But even little children must have an opportunity to investigate the world by themselves. It is good if a mother can sometimes watch from a distance. On the other hand, there are instances when even grown-ups are in need of a genuine mother, when all else fails.

There is a particularly impressive image of this latter example in the mother of Leminkainen in the Finnish national epic *Kalevala*. This youthful hero is a tireless suitor. After a great effort he gets himself a beautiful young wife. Nevertheless he cannot resist journeying north to woo Pohjola's daughter. Here he meets with great danger, is mortally wounded and, in the extremities of death, calls on his mother:[31]

'O my mother who hast borne me
and hast nurtured me with labour,
would that thou might'st know, and hasten
to thy son who lies in anguish.
Surely thou would'st hasten hither
To my aid thou then would'st hasten,
To thy hapless son's assistance,
At the point of death now lying,
For indeed too young I slumber,
And I die while still so vital.'

His call for help is unheard. He dies, and his corpse is hacked to pieces and thrown into the river of death.

Back home they hear that he is no longer alive, and his mother undertakes what neither his young wife nor any of his loved ones will do. She sets out to look for him. Eventually she comes to the river of death whose waterfalls have scattered the pieces of Leminkainen's corpse. She weeps aloud, but not for long, for she soon hurries off to the smith and asks him to make a long rake. Then she wades through the water and rakes together all the pieces of her dead son. She puts him together, calls on good and helpful spirits and, thanks to their magic power, she succeeds in creating him anew. Finally he has everything except speech. So she sends the bee up to the ninth heaven to fetch ointment from Jumala, the greatest of the gods, and this she smears over him, giving him life and speech:

> Thus did Leminkainen's mother
> cause her son with all her efforts
> to resume his old appearance,
> and ensured that in the future
> he should even be superior,
> yet more handsome than aforetime;
> And she asked her son thereafter
> was there anything he needed?

I know no more beautiful description of the endurance, dependability and magic of a mother's love. If a child is able to experience it without interruption throughout childhood then later on in life these same forces will turn into inner security, hope and confidence.

Matriarchal Cults and Matriarchy

> Hitherto it has been women who sustained the
> earth's mystical meaning. If they were not here the
> spirit would have merely a desert to preside over.
>
> *Maurice Maeterlinck*

In the history of religions, mythology, and civilization in
general, there is no more wonderful, infinite and inspiring
theme than that of matriarchal cults. They mirror cares,
hopes and ways of thinking that have been a concern of
humanity since time immemorial, especially as they are
associated with the *mystery of life*, and the perpetual renewal
of the life of human beings, animals, nature, the earth—
even in fact of the whole cosmos. Motherhood has been
worshipped in cults for at least 32,000 years, and is
therefore the oldest of ancient traditions, and one in which
we are hard pressed to distinguish between religion and art.
As mother cults are obviously *universal*, so the voices of all
nations, whether known to us or anonymous, of every skin
colour and from every continent, mingle within them as in
one great living symphony. Each nation has immortalized
its own creative contribution in these cults.[32]

When the Czech scholar of matriarchal traditions, Otakar
Nahodil, whose words these are, fled Czechoslovakia in 1966
and took up a professorship in Freiburg, Germany, he found
that the theme of 'mother cults' was not only considered of
little interest but was not even quite 'presentable' in academic

circles. The only acceptable way of presenting it at the time was in the form of depth psychology.

This began to change from the 1970s onwards. Research on matriarchy was now 'in', especially in feminist circles. However this tended to lead to distortion of the facts due to wishful thinking. This was still more likely since feminine predominance is known to have existed in prehistoric times, but little hard evidence from those times has survived. It is therefore not solely due to sexist attitudes on the part of historians that we have heard so little about it. For the most part we have had to rely on inferences drawn from the myths or rituals of ancient cultures that still survive in some form today. But what evidence we have speaks clearly enough:

> In Eurasia—from Santander to Lake Baikal in southern Siberia, from northern Italy to the Rhine—in any of the existing documents of antiquity men scarcely figure at all. On the other hand, across this whole area, depictions of female figures abound, principally in the form of miniature statuettes (4–22 cm high), but also very occasionally in reliefs of monumental conception.

These corpulent figurines are usually of pregnant women of a mature age. The head and the limbs are only indicated whilst the body, breasts, buttocks and sexual organs are well developed. According to Nahodil these figures do not arise from erotic desire, as people previously mistakenly presumed, nor are they fertility idols or goddesses—neither the 'great goddess' nor the 'great mother'—but are simply mothers: pregnant women, mothers of mothers, grandmothers, ancestral mothers, mothers of the tribe and the clan, and mythical female ancestors reaching back to antiquity, who were regarded as ever-present:

Among many nations living far apart and mostly without contact with one another—for instance the Lapps on the one hand and the South American Tupi Red Indians on the other—we find a number of variants of the same idea, namely, that everything in the world has its own mother. There are mothers of rivers, of trees and of rocks. Nature spirits are often called mothers.

We can also call these spirits elemental beings, for all the elements were regarded as motherly. Amongst a great many tribes and peoples we find a veneration of fire. The fireplace was both the centre of the home and of the cult. It had to be constantly fed, for that was where the fire mother lived. In the *Kalevala*, the elements of air and water are portrayed especially beautifully as the mother principle in the figure of the mother of Vainamoinen. The cult of 'mother earth' did not flourish until later. There are a great number of caves in the depths of the earth, once used for ritual, that witness to this. It is interesting to see that an elemental water being of ancient heathen times actually found its way into the Christian Church: a water nymph suckling her young is a figure frequently seen on Romanesque capitals.

A number of folk tales tell of a hero or heroine visiting the mother of the sun, of the moon or of the wind. For instance, this passage occurs in a Bulgarian fairy tale ('The Unborn Girl'):[33]

In a short while he reached the garden and came to the gates of the sun court. The gates were shut. He knocked three times with his middle finger and the gates opened, and a tall and stately old lady with white hair came towards him. She was surprised to see him.

'Good day, mother of the sun,' said the king's son.

'Good day to you young man,' answered the white-haired old lady. 'No human beings ever come here, my son, yet as you have called me "the mother of the sun" come in and tell me what brings you here.'

We can assume that versions such as this one are older than stories in which the hero or heroine simply visits the sun, moon or wind. The same applies to fairy tales in which somebody visits the devil in hell and the first person he meets is the devil's grandmother.

The Fates are also a motherly element. We meet these in fairy tales too, for instance in the 13 fairies in 'Briar Rose'.

All these motherly elemental beings were later incorporated into the figures of goddesses in patriarchal times, or they survived in the occult cults of folk religions.

In Christianity, the tradition of mother worship turns into Mary worship. The Virgin Mary often took the place of ancient mother goddesses. She was worshipped in many cave sanctuaries. People asked for her help with infertility, and customs arose that are a direct continuation of ancient fertility cults. For instance, on the island of Rhodes, childless women go on a pilgrimage to the mountain of Tsambika to visit a miraculous Mary icon. If they can, they climb the precipitous mountain barefoot to pray in the chapel at the summit. To enhance the power of prayer they can spend the night in a cell attached to the chapel, an ancient tradition corresponding to the healing sleep in the ancient sanctuaries of Asclepius.

The image of the Egyptian goddess Isis with her boy Horus is a forerunner of the Madonna with the Jesus child. We have already observed that this picture shows a transition from old matriarchal cultures to patriarchal ones. Erich Neumann writes about this in his book on the origins of consciousness:[34]

One of the important functions of the (good) Isis is to renounce her matriarchal dominance which can still be clearly seen in the original matriarchal pharaohs of Egypt. Isis' struggle for the legitimacy of her son Horus is typical of this self-renunciation in favour of patriarchy. Whilst otherwise the sons were always (i.e. in a matriarchal system) the sons of their mother, it is precisely this recognition of Osiris' fatherhood of Horus that Isis now fights for, for Horus is to take over the heritage of patriarchy from his father. This then establishes the basis of descent for Egyptian pharaohs who call themselves 'sons of Horus'.

Ancient Indian wisdom speaks of the 'Dark Age' (Kali Yuga) beginning around 3000 BC, i.e. at the beginning of the Egyptian cultural epoch. Anthroposophy also points to the radical change of consciousness that took place at this time. The ancient instinctive clairvoyance of humankind was then gradually extinguished. The capacity to find one's ego in an encounter with the outer world—which can be regarded as a masculine impetus—grew ever stronger from then on. This was an evolutionary necessity. We have seen that Isis herself brought about the transition to patriarchy. Without the extinguishing of clairvoyance or disappearance of the wisdom given as intuitive revelation, human beings would have remained eternally immature. They would have been dependent on the leadership of the gods, without the opportunity to develop individual freedom.

Humanity stands at a point of transition once more. The kind of consciousness that is directed solely to the external, material world culminated in the nineteenth century. It became increasingly obvious that here humanity had come up against a boundary.

Rudolf Steiner points to 1899 as the decisive year when the Age of Darkness was succeeded by the Light Age. From now on the feminine element, which had to remain in the background for long ages, acquires an entirely new significance as a cultural factor. It does not do so, however, by renewing an ancient matriarchy but by developing a new inwardness that has to be found in one's own inner being in the encounter with the outer world, thus uniting the masculine and the feminine element. From an evolutionary and historical perspective, therefore, it is very fitting that the beginning of women's emancipation falls in the last third of the nineteenth century. The comprehensive book on 'Matriarchy' written in the nineteenth century by the Basel law historian Johann Jakob Bachofen (1815–87) was a kind of preparation for a new assessment of the feminine.[35]

As motherhood and mother cults were in ancient times associated with the most sacred mysteries and religious rites this also presupposed legal priority for women, or matriarchy.

Bachofen, in his time, met with little understanding for his research. He could have had every success if he had chosen any subject but this one. As it was, the absence of understanding was mostly silent, at the best sympathetic, sometimes it came as outright rejection and scorn. Yet he pursued the work with determination. The book was published in 1861, and a second edition appeared in 1897, after which it sank into oblivion until it was newly published in 1948, and has been much quoted by feminists ever since.

Bachofen was not fighting to improve the social status of women, but was an academic with a strong sense of justice. He lived in good middle-class patriarchal circumstances, and did not attempt in the least to reform them. The fact that many details of his research are now out of date does not in any way diminish their value. His discovery of matriarchy has not lost any of its importance. Until his time the mono-gamous, patriarchal family was regarded in the West as the natural state of affairs. However irrelevant the idea of the legal ascendancy of women may seem at first sight, once we have been alerted to the fact we can still discover remains of old social forms of this type. For instance, on the island of Rhodes it is still the case that a young man from an agricultural district expects his fiancée to contribute a house to the marriage. Even after the marriage the wife remains the owner of it as long as she lives with her husband. We are reminded here of the words of Genesis: 'Therefore shall a man leave his father and his mother, and cleave to his wife' (Genesis 2:24). It is put this way and not the other way round.

In Rhodes a man has consequently to provide for the building of houses for his daughters. Nowadays the daugh-ters' houses are more often built while the children are still small. They are then let to tourists in order to cover some of the outlay—an interesting example of the merging of ancient cultures with modern circumstances!

All these observations and historical investigations are important, and one can feel inwardly strengthened and confirmed as a woman by the thought that there were times when women were predominant.

On the other hand, these considerations add very little to our perception of the tasks of women today. The significance of women in ancient times was based entirely on the function associated with their sex, and this is just what the modern woman, who is striving for self-discovery, wants to leave behind. The archetypal image of the feminine points to abundance in both body and soul; to the acquisition of wealth and possessions and the capacity to give based on this.

The woman was the owner and guardian of possessions, the man the earner. Women today, however, do not want to identify themselves either with the voluptuous ideal of beauty of the Stone Age nor can they fall back on house possession as a foundation of their identity. What they are endeavouring to acquire—individualization and the right to earn—are the very same qualities that have been acquired by men in the patriarchal period of history. It is essential to take this direction, yet we also have to realize that these are specifically *not* feminine characteristics.

All the external attributes of former times, such as possessions and physical fertility, have over the centuries become inward qualities. Of these female attributes, the emotional wealth of mother love is the one that has most clearly survived. Mother love is a gift of nature arising first of all instinctively. We could probably say that it is the loveliest of all the instincts.

As recently as the 1960s women who became mothers accepted and acknowledged the motherly instinct as self-evident. Since then it has begun to deteriorate, along with all other instincts. We have now arrived at the point where its existence is denied altogether in radical feminist circles. This will probably become ever truer in future. However, this does not mean we should infer that such a power has never existed. By repudiating the motherly instinct one denies to women of former times their most prized capacity. We have arrived, as it were, at the lowest point. No wonder a lot of young women feel this and suffer because of it, but can find no remedy because they do not know what underlies it. The only escape they can find at present is to adopt men's way of life, because this is the only way to gain any respect.

We now come to the question of whether it is right that in

the twenty-first century, i.e. in an age when new significance has to be attached to feminine qualities, we should begin by excluding motherly qualities from our scope.

Must the mother instinct disappear altogether before something new can arise? And what will this new element be? On the other hand, can the mother instinct be preserved at all? Nostalgic idealization of motherhood is certainly not a way forward. Finding the right stance towards 'the mother within us' must become a fundamental issue for every female human being, for the future of humanity depends on the mothers of the future.

The Mother Instinct:
The Forbidden Chamber

A riddle: The brother is white and the sister is black.
Every morning the brother kills his sister, and every
evening the sister kills her brother, yet they never
die. The answer: The day is white. He is the brother
of the black night. Every morning at sunrise the day
kills the night, his sister. Every evening, at sunset,
the night kills the day, her brother. Yet day and
night never die.

From a French fairy tale from Gascony[36]

In her book tracing the history of mother love,[37] Elisabeth
Badinter tries to show that it is altogether an invention of the
sentimental eighteenth century. She goes to great lengths to
compile documents to show how children were neglected
and maltreated in past times, going on to say that 'the myth of
spontaneous mother love' did not arise until after 1760, and
that around this time a completely new mother image of care
and devotion was established as a 'test of self-sacrifice which
many women actually still did not rise to'. In the nineteenth
century, women increasingly had to take on the whole task of
children's education, and in the twentieth century they had
to cope with psychological aspects of child development as
well. Mothers were now held responsible for their children's
difficulties. This author describes women as longing to
develop their personality and being tired of the role of
motherhood; and thus they have no feelings of guilt but
instead a tendency to bitterness.

None of this is wrong, but is very one-sided. The fact that children of the lower classes often had difficult lives had to do with the prevailing state of destitution. Due to the mismatch between population density and agricultural productivity, especially between the sixteenth and the middle of the nineteenth centuries, the masses were fated to be impoverished. In addition, there was social discrimination against the poor. Poverty was increasingly regarded as a moral defect, as laziness. Children who begged were driven away. We find a striking example of the misery of the poor in the tragic story of the childhood of Karl May, who became famous, infamous even, for his Red Indian stories.[38] He came from a family of weavers in the Erz Mountains. He describes his mother, who suffered a lifetime of acute poverty and hunger, and also had a hot-tempered husband, as a veritable saint who sacrificed everything for her children. There are many such instances. Of course there were also women whose misery and despair made them thoroughly hard-hearted.

Elisabeth Badinter's research is, moreover, confined to France, the very first country in which, in the seventeenth century already, a women's emancipation movement arose. Called 'Les Precieuses', this formed among the nobility during the Age of Enlightenment. Their aims were to become educated and reject the traditional role of motherhood. This inspired Molière to write his comedy *Les Femmes Savantes,* in which Armande says:

What a small role you play in this great world
While domesticity keeps you enthralled.
Can your imagination not rise higher than
Rocking your babes and cooking for your man?

It seems that the mother instinct crumbled sooner in France
than in other countries. This is perhaps why the prominent
champion of women's rights, Simone de Beauvoir, has no
understanding whatsoever for women who feel torn between
a profession and motherhood. She did not believe motherliness to be a natural instinct at all, but an acquired one, and
she probably never felt the longing for a child.[39]

In the case of women who have not developed the masculine side of their nature so strongly, things are different.
Quite apart from any psychological theories, unprejudiced
observation shows that the so-called mother instinct is rooted
far more deeply in females than the sex urge. On the whole a
girl's imagination dwells at an earlier age on the children she
would like to have and cherish than on the male partner
needed to have them.[40] Modern enlightenment unfortunately mostly only considers the biological facts, and not
subtler, emotional nuances. So motherhood is no longer
presented as a fulfilment of female existence but more as a
misfortune that women should do their utmost to avoid.
Contraceptives are one of the first things a young girl hears
about on the subject.

Sex and motherhood are among the deepest mysteries of
existence. A girl who is awakening sexually is like the girl
described pictorially in stories about 'the forbidden chamber'.
The best known of these stories is the Grimms' fairy tale 'The
Mary Child',[41] but this one in particular has lost some of its
original archetypal quality in its Christian form. The prevailing motif of the girl being saved from death by confessing
her misdeed is not typical, and probably derives from the
Catholic practice of the forgiveness of sins at confession. In
the more archaic form of the story, the girl's secretiveness is
actually rewarded.

This is true, for instance, in a fairy tale from the Danube region called 'At the Black Lady's Castle'.[42] It tells of a poor cottager who has seven children. When the eldest daughter is 12 years old the father tries to find work for her. He meets a black woman who rewards him handsomely for leaving the girl with her, and promises that she will be treated well. She takes the girl to a castle containing a hundred rooms. She is given all the keys, with the injunction to tidy and clean one room every day, in succession. But she must on no account go into the hundredth room. If she performs this service for three years she will, she is promised, make her fortune.

The girl obeys. She finds everything she needs in the castle and does her work conscientiously. But, as we can well imagine, two weeks before the three years are up she can contain her curiosity no longer, and peeps into the forbidden chamber.

What does she see there? Her mistress, the black woman, undergoing transformation. She is almost totally white: only the tips of her toes are still black.

The girl slams the door again quickly, and when she is called to account she remains silent. Her mistress banishes her from the castle. She finds herself back in a wild wood, scantily clad. There she lives until a king's son chances to find her while hunting, takes her home with him and makes her his wife. In the following years she brings three children into the world. Each time, the black woman appears soon after she has given birth, and asks: 'What did you see in the hundredth room?' She stubbornly remains silent. The black woman takes the children away from her, making her the first time deaf, the second time dumb and the third time blind. The young queen is slandered and accused of killing her children, and eventually she is condemned to death. When she is already tied to the stake, the black woman appears again and asks the question for the last time. When the queen still persists in her silence, the black woman is redeemed and becomes radiantly white, extinguishes the fire and returns the children to her.

A number of aspects of this fairy tale are important for our theme. In all the versions of this story the girl is about the same age—puberty—when she is removed from her parents and has to prove herself in service. Her new world is very much larger than the world of her childhood, but it is an inner world—a large castle with many rooms. One could say that she discovers her inner life, her life of soul. She suddenly discovers a variety of new sides to life and she has to cultivate them. However, she knows there is one room that is forbidden her, and this is the unique sphere of the female figure whom she serves.

She enters nevertheless and discovers *the mother in herself.* The fact that she is initially black means that she is still in the dark realm of the unconscious. However, in the process of growing up in service the young girl has been unknowingly working on the transformation of this figure in her. If daylight enters too soon into this realm, development is disturbed and initially weak and susceptible.

In all ancient cultures some things were 'taboo'—too holy to be spoken of. They were not to be desecrated. In Jutland this kind of taboo surrounded Nerthus, goddess of conception, whom people were not permitted to set eyes on. The black woman, too, is connected with the holy mystery of something coming into being. The girl saw the revered figure of the woman still in the process of transformation. She was deeply shaken and resolved to remain silent.

In a commentary on this story, Ingrid Riedel writes:[43]

Instead of punishing a child for telling a lie out of fear, a conscious and resolute silence is here rewarded. We notice that by keeping silent and saying 'No' the young woman breaks the spell of a tremendous force that has been lurking in the background. This shows us that the Danube fairy tale is the oldest and the most powerful of these tales, precisely because it is a version that offends our modern consciousness, yet in which we do not simply find values similar to the present times but can rediscover ancient ones.

The girl proves to have respect for the sacredness of the taboo even though she has violated it: an attitude people had in earlier times with regard to the gods and their commands.

There is, moreover, another variation of this story in which the figure in the chamber actually exacts a promise of silence from the girl.

Of course, the first taboo to be violated is the opening of the forbidden door. The question as to what might have happened if this had not occurred is on a par with the question of how human evolution would have turned out if Adam and Eve had not eaten the apple. The expulsion into the forest is comparable to the expulsion from paradise. The girl feels stripped and bare, and tries to hide in a gloomy, vegetative world, a forest that is certainly not a modern park but a sort of primeval jungle.

Every young person between the ages of 12 and 20 becomes acquainted in some way with this forest. A sense of being left naked often arises, of being unable to bear close scrutiny. Many youngsters appear to be deaf, dumb and blind during the difficult age of puberty. The fact that the young queen loses her children immediately after giving birth to them could possibly be interpreted as meaning that she is not yet ready for motherhood. She must first of all undergo a trial of will, a test of endurance that is far harder than the first one, and brings her close to death.

What kind of being is the black woman? It would be absolutely wrong to invoke anything connected with racism here. She is clearly a mother figure; in an 'inner' rather than outward sense. The external mother figure would be the girl's own mother, while the inner one is the mother the girl herself can become in the future. After all, the black woman later assumes the role of mother for the girl's children when she takes them from her. She is black because she is still in the night realm of the soul and has not yet been 'realized'. Evolution always progresses from the dark and fecund realms of unconsciousness towards the light of consciousness (quite irrespective of race and skin colour). What lies hidden in the lap of the future thus gradually rises increasingly into the light.

It is not a good idea to snatch things too soon from the night of unconsciousness and expose them to the light of day. Human beings need the regenerating force of night to sustain their life processes. It is not for nothing that day and night alternate in a salutary way.

In a Slovenian version of this tale, instead of a black woman who is found in the forbidden chamber, it is 'Mary, the Accursed', rocking on a fiery swing, as Ingrid Riedel tells us.[44] She is cursed because she has been banished from the realm of day consciousness with which she is nevertheless connected, as the name implies. She is like a shadow of the light-filled Mary. Ingrid Riedel says of this tale that:

...this rocking in the forbidden chamber restores the equilibrium that had been lost, bringing things back to the right path, in which they rock backwards and forwards forever.

And all this takes place:

...in contact with fire, which is an element of transformation, as is well known to alchemists, and is the force through which our consciousness must be changed and redeemed.

In another fairy tale (from the Harz region) we hear of a father whose daughter is abducted by a 'green mermaid'. He searches for her, and finds her in a little house in the woods. She is sitting on a throne in front of the mermaid who is surrounded by gnomes. He takes his daughter back home again. She has, meanwhile, become so beautiful during her stay in the house in the woods that the king's son wants her to become his wife.

A girl who has discovered 'the mother within', who has awoken to awareness of her sexuality, becomes more attractive, more 'beautiful'.

The house in the woods apparently has a similar function to the forbidden chamber, for the further course of the tale is very similar to 'The Black Woman'. In this story the mermaid asks the young woman on each occasion, 'Did you see me in my distress?', to which she answers, 'Dearest mother, I did not see you!'

In this formulation it is quite clear that the chamber is forbidden or that at least what is seen in it must not be spoken of, because the person who is in there is in distress, is suffering growing pains. The early stage of growth must remain hidden, like the sprouting seed under the soil or the embryo growing within the body of the mother. This is a law of growth.

There is also a 'right time' for getting to know one's own sexuality. It should not be discovered—which means put to use—too early. Being silent about it is therefore often better than discussing it excessively. The right time psychologically is considerably later than physical maturity. Putting it pictorially, girls must first of all have concluded their encounter with the inner mother before they are really ready to embark on sex. In some cases this point comes surprisingly late (about the mid-twenties).[45]

In this type of fairy tale the encounter with the 'inner mother' always takes place *first* and the encounter with the sexual partner later. Where it is the other way round, i.e. when a girl is wooed by a man who then brings her into contact with the forbidden chamber for the first time (e.g., 'Bluebeard', 'Odds and Ends Bird') the man is a depraved person and the room contains a blood bath. This confirms the view that in female development motherliness precedes sexuality.[46]

There is a tremendous amount of misunderstanding in this area. Of course it is tempting for young girls to open the 'forbidden chamber' prematurely. But their attitude to sex is often determined far more by curiosity than by need. Or they lack the patience to wait for the right moment. In my opinion the differences between the way men and women feel with regard to sex have not been studied nearly clearly enough. Fashion plays into this realm, too, and young people in particular tend to imitate the suggestive patterns of public opinion. The following is an interesting example of the misunderstandings we have alluded to.

As part of a sex research project, a group of women between 18 and 45 were asked what motivated them to have their first sexual contact with a man; and the men were asked what they thought their partners' motive was. About 73 per cent of the men thought it was desire (libido), 5 per cent thought it was fear of losing their partner. In the case of the women it was exactly the opposite: 6 per cent said 'desire' and 76 per cent fear of otherwise losing their partners.[47] Can we speak of emancipation of female sexuality if the fear of having a child is merely replaced by another fear? Previously, if a woman put forward the argument that she did not yet want a child, a responsible partner would accept this and not interpret it as lack of love. Nowadays many girls feel compelled to surrender in order to keep the man they love.

The wisdom of fairy tales illumines much of the background to the differences between men and women. The story of the redemption of the black woman describes a test of will leading to the threshold of death, and in this respect corresponds to the test of vaulting the bull in Minoan civilization. In this form it is always the girl who has to undergo the trial.

The soul chaos which both boys and girls have to go through when they awaken to the world of desires during puberty is obviously of quite a different nature for the male than for the female sex. A man longs for fulfilment through the woman, the woman for fulfilment through motherhood.[48]

There is also a type of fairy tale that describes a trial for the male hero, namely, the 'redemption of the black virgin'. This also has to do with extremely difficult trials, the so-called nights of agony. An example of this is the Grimms' story 'The Prince who Wasn't Afraid of Anything'. The King's son has to spend three nights in the great hall of an enchanted castle. Every night at midnight a host of small demons come to beat and torment him. All the while he has to hold his tongue and not be afraid. One thing they cannot do is to kill him. Every morning a black virgin enters and tends his wounds with the water of life. The first morning her feet have become white, the second morning she is white to her fingertips, and the third morning she is totally redeemed and as white and as fair as the day. This story, too, is not so much concerned with deeds as with patient endurance and the bearing of pain and sorrow. The story reminds us of the temptation of St Anthony, and no doubt has a similar meaning.

A man has to go through trials to acquire a wife, a girl in order to be fit for motherhood.

With the help of fairy-tale images this chapter has explored how mother love is a deeply embedded instinct in females, a fact that actually requires no proof. Though there may be women nowadays who have almost wholly lost the mother instinct, there are a great many who still possess it and in whom it lovingly comes to life at the first glimpse of the child they have given birth to, or at the latest when they take it in their arms to suckle it.

We would be justified in asking whether it is appropriate nowadays to invoke old instincts that also exist in the animal world. Is it not part of human evolution that such things fade away?

They certainly will fade, but this can happen in two ways. We can passively await their disappearance, in which case a valuable natural force will be lost. Or we can transform it by consciously nurturing and enhancing it. Rudolf Steiner chose mother love as an example when describing how egotism can develop into altruism. Initially there is certainly something egotistic about mother love. The child is loved as a personal possession, as though it were part of the mother's own body. In course of time the loving care extends to a number of people, to a whole family; but this may still be called egotism—family egotism. However, if the family does not close itself off but opens up to let others in, these can also share its warmth.

The social qualities a woman learns within her own family—motherly care and attention—can eventually serve an ever-wider circle. Thus an instinct can gradually grow into a real force of love that is no longer exclusive, wants nothing for itself, does not have the feeling of 'that's mine' any more, but has become universal, human love.

The Gateway to Motherhood

Conception

Whenever we breathe as one,
With our hearts beating close together,
Unborn souls seek to steal their way
Into life on the crest of our desire.

Playing and kissing and intimate abandon,
In the inexhaustible, unseeing night!
The morning calls us to fresh joys
But a new being comes to light:

And now as we gaze eye to eye,
Do you feel what is starting within us?
A new sun is urging us to say
Whether we're one with its will's radiance.

Hans Carossa

In olden times human life was regulated and accompanied by rites and traditions, which gave people's consciousness an external support. Whenever a new step or stage in life arrived, rites focused their attention on it. A festival marked the advent of the new and the departure of the old, whether it was the seasons of the year, weddings, baptisms or funerals.

It is characteristic of our time that, even in a quite external sense, we have ever fewer doors and thresholds. People prefer one space to lead unnoticeably into another, doors to open soundlessly and automatically, escalators to take us effortlessly from one floor to the next. People like to slip in similar fashion from one life situation to the other. They think they have more freedom if they set up no dividing lines but always leave various possibilities open. In fact the reverse is true. By allowing things to take their own course we can, unwittingly, be subject to external compulsion. If we do not make intentional choices of our own, new situations are forced upon us.

Looking at life as a whole, the gates of birth and death are the greatest dividing lines; but even here suppression mechanisms are at work. People would like to ignore death for as long as possible. After the birth of a child people often try to get back as quickly as possible to the way they lived before.

In former times a wedding was also a woman's departure from her parental home and often the beginning of the first pregnancy. The bride's feelings were a mixture of joy and pain. Many customs brought home to her that there was no going back across this threshold. There was the custom of 'stealing the bride', the last echoes of which we see in the husband carrying his wife over the threshold. In Greek times the axle of the chariot in which the bride had been taken to the bridegroom's house was burnt, so that she might never think of returning to the parental home. The custom in many places of the bride weeping also emphasized the finality of the departure. Nowadays this is just what people want to avoid. They do not think there is much difference whether they are married or not. They have usually already left their parents' home, and motherhood has either already begun or can be postponed.

Yet we could save ourselves some heartache if, when we started living with a sexual partner, we were to place more emphasis on this as the beginning of a new stage in our life. People often believe that by living together as a sort of provisional experiment they are preparing themselves in the best way for the possibility of marriage. This is true only in a very limited sense. It is, of course, a way of finding out whether one's partner is selfish or not, and whether he or she has any little irritating habits. Most marital problems are caused by ridiculously tiny details. However, this is building our life from below upwards, which applies to houses, rather from above downwards, which is the right principle for spiritual creations.[49]

The dividing line created by entering into a life partnership is often more highly charged for a woman than for a man. Not only does she frequently assume greater responsibility for shared housekeeping,[50] but the question of whether to have or to avoid a pregnancy is one of existential dimensions.

It is an interesting language phenomenon that almost all nouns that can be both masculine and feminine have a masculine stem (manager) and can be made feminine by adding an extra ending (manageress), with the exception of the word 'bride' which needs an addition to become 'bridegroom'. In past times, when language was still in more creative flux, this reflected people's view that the bride was more important than the bridegroom.

Nowadays, living together does not need to include pregnancy. The freedom women and girls have acquired over the past 30–40 years through various methods of contraception enable women to have sexual intercourse without physical consequences, just like men. Yet this consequence, this possibility of pregnancy, is part of the very nature of the female body. To put it bluntly, we are living in an age in which women are trying to emancipate themselves from their female body by acquiring freedoms that are of a masculine nature. If this is done by meddling with the hormone balance, the full scale of damaging effects this may have on the female organism is hard to quantify. A further consequence is that men have acquired, in addition, the freedom not to have to consider the receptivity of the female body, for contraception is possible and abortion now widely available.

There can, of course, be no universally valid rules for when and how a partnership should begin. The removal of outer constraints has given us the opportunity to make decisions in freedom, which is a great gain. But deciding in freedom does not mean doing something because others do it. It is much more a matter of being conscious of the various possibilities and their consequences. In feminist circles marriage and motherhood are often called a 'trap' for the woman; that is, a situation she neither intends nor wants to be in. If a marriage is a trap it is not the fault of marriage itself, so much as the couple entering into it who lack awareness of what it will really mean.

If the couple have come to a free decision to live together for life, this decision can be confirmed and reinforced by expressing it publicly in the setting of a church wedding. This, of course, applies only if the couple are religiously inclined, so that a ceremony of this kind means something to them, and is not just a matter of form.[51] It should never be done as mere convention or to please someone else. The motive for a church wedding can be as sign and symbol of the couple's own strengthened awareness and that of the congregation. It is a way to make everyone aware of the importance of the event. In course of time people's consciousness may be strong enough to do without marking the occasion outwardly. At present we are still a long way from that.

In the marriage ritual of the Christian Community, a

movement for religious renewal,[52] the bride and bridegroom
do not, as is customary, take an oath of fidelity, but say 'yes' in
answer to whether the decision for this life partnership is a
spiritual one—i.e. has arisen from the individual freedom of
each of them. During the preparatory work and discussion
prior to the wedding this can give rise to deep self-reflection,
for the decision is thereby lifted far above the mundane level.
The meaning of any festival is, of course, to lift us above our
everyday lives, so that a new impulse can enter us.

A marriage can turn our minds in two directions. Looking
into the past we can say: 'We believe the two of us have a
connection through our destiny. Our meeting is a kind of re-
encounter.'

In one of his stories Adalbert Stifter describes the first
meeting of a young man and girl in the following words:

> Her entry into my life worked like a chink in the fabric of
> my thoughts. I cannot say I love her; for one can only love
> what one knows—yet it is as though innumerable years
> ago on another star she was once my wife.[53]

Not everyone experiences this past aspect so intensely. The
other aspect, the future one, is actually more important. It
consists of an absolutely down-to-earth decision: 'We want to
lift our relationship and our love from a merely soul level into
the realm of decisions and responsibilities we ourselves choose
to take. We have the will to be faithful to one another. Our
partnership is something other people can rely on. It will be a
basis for the children we hope to have. In our decision to have
children we will integrate ourselves into the whole of
humanity as its smallest social community. We do not want to
cut ourselves off from the rest of the world, but we want our
family to be open to all those who find their joy and help in it.'

The Christian aspect of marriage is to wish to shape one's destiny so that it contributes to the general welfare of humanity. This goes beyond a desire for personal happiness. And while it may be an ideal that is seldom realized, yet that is surely no reason not to try. It can be a guiding light to us, acting as a constant reminder.

In Rudolf Steiner's first Mystery Play *The Portal of Initiation* the two main characters, Maria and Johannes Thomasius, see in a powerful imaginative picture that their union has the blessing of the spiritual world. This experience strengthens their conviction of how closely their lives are connected. They experience a kind of 'spiritual ritual' of which any earthly ritual can only be a reflection. Yet even at this high spiritual level things can go wrong. The image still has to become reality:

> To see a picture has been granted
> Of what the future holds in store for you
> When you, unscathed, have passed the greatest trials.
>
> Beholding here the ultimate reward
> Of unremitting effort is no sign
> That you are at the end of your endeavour.
> You have seen but a picture which your will
> Alone can turn into reality.

The sacrament of marriage, in a modern sense, can do no more and no less than highlight this image of partnership. Its realization is not assured by the ceremony, which acts only as a kind of stimulus to the will; in fact this is what gives it its religious character. It makes a difference to a partnership whether you begin by saying, 'We want to give mutual support to our shared will,' or whether you think, 'Let us leave things as open as possible, so as to allow us to separate more easily.'

The importance and significance of a partnership between a man and a woman lies in the fact that it implies more than an agreement between an I and a You. The following verses by Carossa express the real essence of this in all its depth and significance: the miraculous fact we have already touched on that the intimate union of two people can produce not only a soul dynamic but actual physical life.

Whenever we breathe as one,
With our hearts beating close together,
Unborn souls seek to steal their way
Into life on the crest of our desire.

Christian Morgenstern also wrote a poem about this, which he called 'Mystery'.

Invisible threads weave
hidden forces between us
bind into one single life
our nights and our days

Thus we grow together
until we wholly glide
beyond ourselves. And over
our heads the eyes

of a third being shine already.

This spiritually real configuration is depicted in one of the stained glass windows at the Goetheanum.[54] Above the man and the woman we see spiritual currents sent downwards by a Janus-headed being seeking to incarnate. It is looking back to earlier forms of existence and also forward to the couple it wishes to join. It is involved in helping the destined meeting to come about between the parents-to-be.

A child is not created by conception. Before birth it plays into the feelings that pass to and fro between man and woman.[55] Rudolf Steiner describes in a lecture how the soul of the child plays a part in the passionate love of its parents.

> If we think this thought through to the end we have to say that a human being on its way into reincarnation certainly has a share in the choice of its parents. In a certain sense the child loves its parents even before conception, and this draws it to them. The parents' love is therefore the response to the child's love. It is the answer to it.[56]

It is important for the man and the woman to be conscious of the existence of this invisible third member in their union and also to talk about it. There are a great many examples of this theme in the book *Children who Communicate Before they are Born*.[57] The dreams and very real feelings which the descending soul invokes should be raised more clearly into consciousness. 'Conception' is not only a physical process but also a soul-spiritual one.

The words 'soul receives soul' resounded like the chiming of bells through a striking dream dreamt by a young woman about to be married. A beautiful woman whom she did not know but felt she had often seen, appeared in the dream, pregnant, and her body was so transparent that the unborn child was clearly visible. A dream of this nature is instructive for motherhood altogether, for it both tells and challenges every expectant mother to be inwardly alert to the soul qualities of the child who is on the way to us.

It is certainly possible to have a fairly clear picture of the character and temperament of a child before he or she has even been born. Searching for a suitable name, provided this is not done over-intellectually and superficially, can put us in the right mood. This kind of perception of the child's being diminishes somewhat in the early days after birth, overlaid by the child's physical appearance.

The constant pressure to 'perform' as well or even better than men has brought women to the point of largely ignoring pregnancy, and as far as possible motherhood as well, as though the whole thing could be fitted in alongside their normal life. This deprives them of important experiences. A mother-to-be should have the time to concentrate in peace on the coming arrival. For both herself and her child it is of great significance how she spends her time, and whether she succeeds in overcoming the sort of inner unrest we all suffer from, and developing a feeling for what is taking place within her.

Our own body—which we know to be the dwelling-place of our soul, and which we think of as our own possession and more or less identify with—suddenly becomes the space in which a process takes place that is at one and the same time both natural and cosmic, and which goes far beyond our own comprehension. A woman can feel 'squeezed out', and the morning sickness many suffer from may have to do with the fact that their own bodies no longer so readily or easily house them.

This kind of sickness is not inevitable, and although I had four children I only know of it from hearsay. On the other hand I remember that at the start of a pregnancy I often felt I was being drawn downwards, as though the earth was sucking me in. In fact this feeling told me I was pregnant before a missing period confirmed it. In those days (the 1960s) people did not feel they had to consult a doctor at once. When I was expecting my fourth child I did not have a medical examination until the fifth month. I just did not feel like telling an outsider of my condition before then.

In any case, the medical aspect of the matter seemed to me of secondary importance. So I had four home confinements. It is more pleasant to stay in one's home surroundings as long as there are no strong reasons against doing so. You feel more at ease and more in control of what happens.

It is obvious that a pregnant woman can initially feel very uncertain about her condition. She is vulnerable and open to any medical suggestions deemed necessary from the medical side, from ultrasound scans to electrodes placed on the child's head. Young mothers should be sufficiently self-assured to resist such things and to remember that a birth is a natural process and not a disorder of some kind. The medical profession has the duty only to help in cases of emergency, and these are the exception.

Fearlessness and confidence are qualities a mother must not allow herself to be deprived of. After all, the birth does not concern her only but also affects the child.

Roman Polanski's film *Rosemary's Baby* was a great shock to many people. It shows a pregnant woman being subjected to psychological manipulation and satanic ritual, so that the child she bears becomes a little devil. The chief method used here is creating panic, apprehension and insecurity in the young woman so that she becomes more and more susceptible to manipulation. After seeing the film it occurred to me that this was the opposite of the legend of Merlin.[58] Merlin was a magician who played a significant role in the King Arthur legends. He was 'the son of the devil and a pure virgin'. The legend tells of a girl who was in such difficulties that she fell into the power of the devil and became pregnant by him. She went into the forest to a wise hermit and asked him for advice. He found shelter for her in an old tower in the depths of the forest where, under the guidance of the hermit she spent the period of her pregnancy quite alone in prayer and inner training. This caused the devil to lose his power over her and also over the child who, although born with devilish traits such as surpassing intelligence and magic powers, used these forces for good because of his mother's influence.

It is fear of the devil that gives him power over us. When we are afraid we expose ourselves to evil forces. But even when there is a tendency to evil there is the possibility of turning it to good, as we see in the Merlin legend.

A mother is in a position to have great influence on her child's future life. This should not alarm us but make us both aware and proud of our responsibility. Even the way a mother bears the birth pains means something for the child. If she can manage without anaesthetic and without crying out this will have an effect on the child's destiny. The birth is usually considered in terms of what the mother undergoes, whilst the child's experience of it is regarded as very much secondary.

At birth both the child *and* the mother cross a threshold. When a woman gives birth she experiences for the first time that being a mother does not only consist of protecting and sheltering but also of pushing out and giving up what was virtually her own possession. This causes pain. Death comes close for a moment, and one begins to understand that one side of femininity, the dark side, has to do with death.

Birth pains are the kind of things that are very quickly forgotten to make way for joy. In fact there is no physical pain that is rewarded in such a wonderful way as this. A new life has begun.

Something new begins, too, in the mother's inner life. First of all there is a feeling of relief at having regained her youthful form. Then she may notice that the pregnant body has been a kind of support, affording not only protection for the child but also for herself. And she feels its loss. The soul's ground has been ploughed up, as it were, by the deep experiences she has been through. Sensitivities that were stunted and crusted over by routine are suddenly very intense. Both troubles, and joys—such as music and poetry—are deeply felt, and she lives close to tears. People often make far too little positive use of this receptivity. There is so much to distract us.

After the birth of his little sister, a three-year-old brother burst into the room and asked: 'Did you see God?' The child had been told that babies came from God, so he was being quite logical in thinking that God would be seen bringing the baby. In fact, a woman can indeed have a threshold experience whilst giving birth, though we are often too pre-occupied with the more biological process to really notice this.

Throughout, the husband is largely a spectator. But his presence is important. It means a lot to the mother to have a loved person present who is not involved in the general bustle of activity. It also means something to have someone there to protect her and the child from undesired medical attention, and share with her any decisions that are necessary. In the weeks that follow it is often not an easy task for the father to show understanding both for the outer and inner difficulties associated with a newly enlarged family, and to see to it that the young mother gets sufficient rest and care. The more interest and empathy he can muster the less superfluous and neglected he will feel. In paintings of the Christmas story,

Joseph may often be allotted a subsidiary role, yet peace and security emanate from him when one sees him sitting in the corner, where he has lit a fire and is heating the broth. In the environment of a birth it is quite right that the husband should have the role of protector.

Birth as a process of renewal affects the woman right down to her physical body; she will never be the same as before. She has a new dignity, since life has called her to be a mother. She has motherhood as a calling irrespective of any other profession she may pursue.

Being a Mother

Welcome, little one!
We do not know you.
We know only that you have come
To be with us here in this dark space.
Sleep, my little brother!

Welcome, little one!
We reach out to you awkwardly
You do not hear us, for the light of heaven
Still trembles round you as you dream.
Sleep, my little brother!

Welcome, little one!
There are many of us here.
One day you will awaken,
See night enfold the silent stars.
Sleep, my little brother!

Welcome, little one!
We glide down.
Our hands as our paths cross,
Will briefly find each other. You ascend!
Sleep, my little brother![59]

However much we have to do with children, we are
invariably touched by the magic surrounding a newborn
baby. It is surely one of the greatest wonders that a human
being entrusts himself to us in such utter helplessness. We
forgive this small being for disturbing our nights and for all
the other trouble he gives us! The joy of being fed, the smiles
and the daily progress are recompense in plenty. Every time

things get difficult we can remind ourselves that this period
does not last long. It will soon be over! And what are a few
days, a few weeks, even a few months compared to a lifetime!

All we need to do is try to stay calm, take time for our child
and create a suitable environment. There is a huge amount of
advice available for coping with infants. Choose what suits
you. The book I like best was an unassuming little volume
from the nineteenth century by Thérèse Schröer. This was
not because of the details, which have been partly super-
seded, but her pervasive warmth and motherly attitude. She
says a mother should give the love of her whole heart to her
children in their first seven years, and their life should be like
a perpetual Christmas. You will never have real contact with
them when they grow up, she says, if you have not had it
when they are small.[60]

How lucky you are if your early childhood conjures up
pictures of warm, harmonious family life! You will know
what strength, confidence and positive outlook you have
from those early years to help you overcome the kind of
difficulties in later life which everyone encounters.

Affluence is not necessary for children to experience their
first years as a perpetual Christmas. Restricted or impoverished circumstances, which are often very disturbing for
parents, upset children surprisingly little. All they need is for
their parents to have a loving attitude both towards one
another and towards their children.

It is the mother who creates the mood of the world her
child lives in. Therefore the child needs her presence; and
although Daddy, Granny or family friends can replace her on
occasion, this should be the exception to the rule.[61]

There is a very sad story about the little boy whose mother
went off to work every morning. He started to make a scene

every day until she came up with the excuse, 'You see, I have to earn the money for your Dinky cars and your sweets!' When she came home she found on her bed a bag of sweets he had begged from his Granny. 'Now you won't have to go tomorrow, will you?' he said.

Does the career you could be doing and the money you could be earning compensate for what the little ones miss through the constant absence of their mother? In addition, the development of a little child is so full of wonder, so packed with unrepeatable scenes, that a mother who cannot experience this is very much to be pitied.

It is obvious that I am pleading for mothers to spend at least the first few years, if possible the whole pre-school period, at home with their children. Of course a child can go to kindergarten, but I do not consider this obligatory. I think of it as something that can be done either if the mother wants it or, more to the point, if the child does. Some children grow up much more happily and harmoniously if they can remain in their home surroundings for the whole of their pre-school life. I can understand how they feel, because when I myself went to the kindergarten, I squeezed through a hole in the hedge and ran home so often that I eventually did not have to go any more. Other children have more need to get out of the house, and like being in larger groups of children. There might also be educational reasons for putting them into a larger compass: only children, for instance, who are the centre of attention at home, and whose social skills may be slower to develop.

If a woman with a career tries to live her life in exactly the same way with a child as she did without one—for instance with the help of her husband, day-care, or a kindergarten— however important her achievement may be, it is very often to the detriment of the child. The tendency nowadays is to place the interests of the mother above those of the child, because she is able to think through and state her needs while the child cannot. If the child does not cry or get ill, we think everything is fine. I cannot sufficiently stress how rewarding both the outer and the inner sacrifices can be which a mother makes in order to be there for her child.

The chance to develop one's individuality and have a lifestyle suited to one's personality is an important part of life for everyone, not only for women. Increasingly the children born nowadays, even within the same family, are very different from one another from the moment of birth. A really individual and therefore 'human' education clearly cannot be provided in big, state institutions, however, but only in small communities: in families or groups of people working on a close-knit basis, where there is someone in a central position with whom the children can get their bearings, and experience the significance of a strong and permanent relationship.[62] Many people today have not had the opportunity to experience this or to have a harmonious childhood, and therefore face the challenge of replacing by their own efforts what destiny has denied them. We don't solve our problems by blaming our own mother for our shortcomings. There are absurd stories like the one of the man in his forties who was told by a psychiatrist that his mother had made big mistakes with him, and that he should confront her. His response was: 'Why should I do that? I get on very well with my mother. Should I risk spoiling our relationship now because of what happened in the past?'

The sensible thing, instead, is to tell yourself that you will do all you can to see that *your* children receive no lasting damage in *their* childhood. To have this as your aim and to do the best you can at the moment, with self-assurance, is more helpful than tormenting yourself with fears and scruples. Many young mothers today suffer from immense insecurity and doubts about their own capacities, especially when they realize how important their task is. This is quite unnecessary. If a mother takes pains to give her child a proper childhood she does not need to reproach herself, even though she sees later on that she could have done one or another thing better. If one is well intentioned and follows one's natural feeling, there is no reason for self-reproach.

It can be very helpful and rewarding to keep a journal of your life with your children. Then, if you have several children, you can compare their development and see what particular characteristics each one has, take an objective look at your own educational approach and also record amusing scenes. It may often not strike you until later just how typical they were for that particular child. Godparents and grand-parents who are keen to follow children's progress love being shown accounts like this.

In child-raising, people often swing from one extreme to the other. Whereas parents used to be too authoritarian, and set themselves up as absolute sovereigns over their children, nowadays they often allow themselves to be ruled by them. The children's interests are certainly a priority, but that is absolutely no reason for letting them tyrannize us—which is actually not in their best interests.

This begins with the baby's feeds. It is certainly good to start by feeding the child when she cries. However, regularity is a blessing for a child, so as soon as possible it is good to find a regular rhythm that suits her, according to which you can then arrange your work. A newborn baby cannot yet dis-tinguish between night and day—but she has to learn to, and therefore you can try to leave out the night feed as soon as possible. Other things do not matter as much. The most important thing is for the child to be surrounded by warmth, and to know she is loved. Love can also mean not allowing everything. Surrounding the child with warmth does not mean attaching the child to you and taking him wherever you go, be it to the supermarket, a lecture or even the cinema. Being a mother means being the one they can always turn to with their questions, problems and joys.

A very old, invalid lady in a large home for the elderly once asked: 'Who is mother here?' On being asked what she meant by that she explained: 'In a house as large as this somebody has to be mother.' Every house, i.e. every social community, needs a centre of warmth, a 'mother'. You could also say that every organism needs a heart. Social structures are not simply an accumulation of people, but a living organism. In earlier times this could even be seen in the architecture of a building: the centre of a house was the hearth and that of the village the church. If modern European housing estates are grouped around a church this is a relic from medieval times, a form without content that, however, still speaks to us, though we overlook the fact that we no longer appreciate the significance of a central focus in the social realm.

In this sense motherhood really is a vocation; it may not be given its full due today, but it most certainly cannot be considered a thing of the past.

Let us form a picture of this profession. Anne Morrow Lindbergh describes it in the following words:

Being a mother means that your interests and duties ray out from the mother instinct in all directions, just like the spokes from the hub of a wheel. The pattern for us is a circle. We must be open in all directions—to our husbands, children, friends, home and the community—and we must register every puff of wind, every call made on us, as sensitively as any taut spider's web. How difficult it is for us to hold the balance between all these opposing tensions, and yet it is essential that we do so for our life to stay in tune.[63]

A mother cannot live for herself alone. She forms a living unity with her husband and children. Even her thoughts have an effect on others, absorbed as they are by her children. If we are attentive we can repeatedly notice that children utter their mother's thoughts, and are also very sensitive to her moods. If Mummy is not well then, sad to say, her children are often insufferable. Similarly, it can happen that if Mummy is reading horror stories or watching TV, a child in a remote bedroom may wake up screaming. We do not notice that these things have a connection, yet doubtless they have.

It is a feminine quality to observe things of this kind and in general have one's finger on the pulse of what occurs between one person and another. This is also something that a mother can intentionally develop. This process going on 'between' and 'below' what is evident cannot be measured, counted or dished out on a plate. This is why it so often appears to be non-existent, which is very frustrating for many women.

'*How* you do things is more important that *what* you do' is a piece of advice from Goethe that applies generally, but quite particularly to a mother's work. This is why you should make the most of the opportunities this vocation offers and, if you are short of time, cut out the housework or prepare a simpler meal, even if you have visitors. After all, the guests will be more aware of the atmosphere in the home than of the dust on the sideboard.

I am not recommending laziness, dirt or untidiness. Although the mother of a large family[64] will not manage without a certain liberality and tolerance, she will nevertheless try to keep the place clean and tidy, and as beautiful as possible in the way she thinks best. The atmosphere of a home is made up of both the things that are in it and also the kind of activity that goes on there, particularly the loving kind as distinct from the 'duty-bound' kind. This is the sort of thing that is meant when 'diligence' is mentioned in fairy tales as a very special virtue. It means relating to the environment in an active way.

As well as taking care of the spatial environment we also have to deal with the element of time in a creative way. This should also be shaped artistically. The younger children are, the more important it is to have a regular rhythm, always giving them their meals and putting them to bed at the same time. This gives the day a firm structure and a certain tranquillity.

Agnes Sapper (1852–1929), who is well known as a writer of children's books, says in a letter:

> I notice every day that there is nothing worse than being in such a hurry that I know I cannot do things properly. Unless I am at ease I cannot be in good spirits, and if one is out of sorts one makes a mess of everything.

This points to something extremely important. You need to be calm to engender a positive frame of mind. A mother's good spirits, cheerfulness and serenity flow out to the whole family, just as her restlessness will undermine the whole atmosphere.

As soon as the children go to school, a mother's round of

duties changes. The moment when the eldest child goes to school can be a big turning point for a mother, even a somewhat painful one. It is like a second birth. This turning point is even greater for the child, of course. He or she will acquire ever more experiences outside the family circle and become increasingly independent.

From this moment on, listening, registering and restoring equilibrium—the qualities that Anne Morrow Lindbergh characterizes as specifically motherly attributes—become even more important. There is a very charming description in Agnes Sapper's beautiful children's book 'The Pfäffling Family' of what happened when a mother was temporarily absent. The father sat down to dinner with his seven children. Very soon he became aware that there was total silence, though they were usually a lively bunch of children who could hardly wait for their turn to speak. Yet mother was rather a quiet, contemplative person whose presence and attentive ear obviously supplied the encouragement for the children to share what was on their mind.

Recent research undertaken at the University of Freiburg[65] on the different way men and women converse showed that women generally listen more actively, which is seen by their interspersed comments such as 'yes', 'good', 'well done!', 'I think so too'. On the whole their contributions to the conversation are shorter and more directly to the point, whereas even in conversation men show somewhat more of a tendency to hold monologues.

This more feminine approach must not be regarded as more positive in every situation, but it certainly encourages conversation at the meal table of a large family, and gives everyone the sense of participating.

In the child's second seven-year period, besides taking

note of what he or she experiences outside the home, providing a greater wealth of family experiences is also of course important: for instance games, telling stories, singing, playing instruments and going on outings and holidays. Going somewhere new and different together can offer a fund of vivid, exciting or happy memories.

If the children's urge to be active oversteps the mark it is right at this age (7–14) to exercise your decisive authority. The children must know that certain rules have to be kept, and this also gives them great security. (Fortunately you often do not find out until later all the things they got up to!)

This is also the age when a mother and father can restrain their instinct for self-sacrifice and get real help by encouraging their children to share in the work. It is of course best to delegate small jobs in a cheerful way rather than waiting until you feel thoroughly frustrated that everything lands on your shoulders all the time.

Teaching ourselves that it is far less important to get household chores quickly out of the way than to enjoy the experience of doing them helps those jobs to seem more interesting to the children, and they will not tire of them so easily. Our own enjoyment—or frustration—with such work naturally communicates itself in non-verbal ways.

When these essential jobs are spread out more over the entire family this enables a mother to take up her own personal interests again, either in the form of a job in the 'outside' world or by doing her own thing at home. Being a mother should not entail suppressing your personal life and interests altogether. When they are older the children judge quite differently the interests you may have put aside for the time being. They respect them and admire the fact that you are not just a house drudge.

A mother needs time to withdraw and come to herself. What she gains from these moments does her good, and therefore the whole family benefits. Quiet times can be tremendously restorative, joyful occasions.

These quiet moments may also give you the creative urge and put you in the right mood to break out of the routine of the ordinary daily pattern by having occasional celebrations, for instance in the form of seasonal festivals. These need re-enlivening in some way, since today they have largely grown very materialistic, and old customs have become empty traditions.[66] Anyone who had the privilege of experiencing 'proper' Christmas festivals in their childhood knows how much this meant for the whole of later life. The grown-ups have the opposite experience: it is the children's joy that makes Christmas so special. In this sense parents receive at least as much from their children as the children do from their parents.

Once we have acquired a taste for this, we can discover other festivals anew or invent some ourselves. A bit of an impetus for this may come from the following 'Letters to Andres', one of a series by Matthias Claudius (1740–1815) which appeared regularly in 'The Wandsbeck Messenger' periodical.[67] He was obvious a genius at inventing festivals, though he was not a mother but a father! And though the letter is couched in antiquated style, it still sparkles. Below are his suggestions:

3 October 1782

New Ideas

I have invented something new, Andres, and I want to pass it on to you hot from the press.

You will know that every well-ordered household celebrates all the special days, and that the father of the family does his family a good turn if he can invent a new one that is satisfactory and acceptable. Thus in addition to the various birthdays and saints' days the two of us have introduced various other festivals, such as the Bud Festival, May Day and Green Tongues, when the first young peas and beans are due to be picked and served up at table.

Summer, and especially spring are of course a very beautiful time of year. This beauty starts from the moment the snows melt and we can see the bare body of the earth again for the first time, and it continues in leaps and bounds until the flowers and leaves have all opened and we stand enthralled, beholding the spring in its full glory. Spring certainly has a great deal to tell us about God and His goodness, for as our friend Fritz says, what touches our hearts must come from the heart. So all the redletter days that fall in spring and summer are fully justified. But although I have often thought we should also do something in autumn and winter, until now I was not sure what to do.

But *we* do not find new ideas, they find *us*, and yesterday, as I went into the garden, holidays were the last thing I was thinking about, when all of a sudden two new festivals shot into my mind: *Little Autumnmas* and *Icicle Friday*, both of which are fun and useful, and lend themselves to being celebrated.

Little Autumnmas is only short, and you celebrate it with baked apples. When the first snows come in autumn—and you must take special care to catch the moment—you take as many apples as there are children and people in the house, and one or two extra in case visitors come, so that nobody goes short, put them in the oven, wait until they are baked, and then eat them. If this is done properly, it is as much fun as it is simple to do. You can imagine all the conversations this leads to, and the number of times people have to peep into the oven.

So that's *Little Autumnmas.*

Icicle Friday needs to be treated quite differently, and it has a very special appeal. You may be thinking that as soon as you see icicles hanging from your roof you can begin celebrating. Far from it. There is much more to it than that. *Icicle Friday* cannot be celebrated at all unless you have a snowman, for which you have to have snow first of all and then a thaw, so that you can make it. When he has been made, and stands in front of your window, it has to freeze again so that the icicles, half an ell long, hang from the roof—neither longer nor shorter. Those are the preliminary conditions, *the conditio sine qua non.* What do you say to that? It is a mighty complicated festival, isn't it? Some winters come and go without our being able to have one of these at all. However, if all the above circumstances apply, and there is no other obvious obstacle, you can begin the festival between 3 and 4 p.m., and, please note, the whole thing has to be done without eating or drinking. After 4 p.m., when it has grown dark, you put a lantern into the snowman's hollow head so that the light shines out through his eyes and his mouth, and then everyone, both great and small, walks to and fro in the room looking out of the window past the hanging icicles at the snowman, each one thinking of his own favourite snowman; and that is the highlight of the festival.

Goodbye my dear Andres, celebrate all the festivals and holy days properly until Christmas really arrives.

Your Matthias

A description of idyllic family occasions such as these fill me with a certain sense of sadness. We often think we simply do not have time for such things. But what Claudius describes involves very little time, and it is the importance you attach to these things and the fun you have with them that makes them festive. It really takes very little time or preparation.

We are unlikely ever to be able to celebrate *Icicle Friday* because the necessary weather conditions are so rare. But that is not the point. It is much more a matter of triggering our own inventiveness. It is interesting to note that Claudius always chooses a natural phenomenon to which he draws his children's attention. It is very important for children (and adults) to follow the course of the year with a sense of wonder about nature. Three 'virtues' of motherhood involve: active engagement with things and love for what one does; being in good spirits and cheerful; and, lastly, following the course of the year with wonder and sensitivity. Together these can form the foundation for harmonious family life.

The Profession of Homemaker

How easy-going it used to be
When the little folk were around!
For if you felt lazy you just lay down
On a couch to take your ease—
Then at nightfall, in a twinkling,
All the little sprites were there:
    Rattling and banging
    And sweeping and rubbing
    And polishing and scrubbing
With a hippety-hop and a broom and a mop.
And ere a lazy-bones awoke
Everything was tidied up!

August Kopisch

Some women think it would be very nice to look after children and bring them up if only there were not all the tiresome housework to do! So we are going to devote a special chapter to it.

Looking after the house is not the hard work it used to be. Most people have a modern home with the usual technical equipment. But this doesn't stop you standing there feeling lonely! Generally speaking, people think a 'housewife's' loneliness is due to the isolation of a small family unit. On the other hand, many historical studies show that extended families in the olden days—consisting of several generations living under one roof—were largely a myth! There were also many small families in those days. It was certainly true that people had more of a group consciousness, felt connected with relatives and neighbours, and often saw one another, and helped one another with particular jobs or at least got together to do them. Unless they were very poor they usually had servants, a cook, a maid, and you can talk to a maid and either praise her or scold her. You cannot do that with a washing machine. On top of this, work done with a machine is less satisfying, because less rhythmically engaging than the productive activities of earlier times, such as spinning, weaving, sewing, harvesting, the preparation and storing of food, right through to the making of candles and soap. And this is where we should ask a question. If you enumerate all the activities that had to be done in a household, you must admit that the people of olden times were extremely industrious. So what is the old story about little folk actually telling us when it says they did the work of 'lazy' people?

Though not written so very long ago, this little poem by August Kopisch (1799–1853) still testifies to a sense for the 'little folk'. It certainly was not the case that as soon as the baker climbed out of bed in the morning the loaves of bread flew into the shop window, carried there by invisible hands. If, however, we allow Kopisch's verses to work on us, with their rattling, banging, and sweeping and rubbing, and polishing and scrubbing, the regular, soothing rhythm could suggest to us that when people were at work in this rhythmic way they were not fully awake! In other words, while engaged in a slow and regular activity they fell into a kind of dream consciousness—we dream, too, if we have to stir something for a long time—and when they awoke the job was done. Who had done it? The person who was asleep? No, they thought someone must have helped them whose sphere of influence was in their subconscious, their instinctual life, and guided their hands. These were the hobgoblins!

However, when the light of waking consciousness shines into this region—when the tailor's wife comes with her lamp—whoops! The little people are off and away, and all that remains is tedious and monotonous work!

The house sprites active in an imponderable way in the processes taking place in different kinds of work were not merely imagined by people of olden times but actually 'seen'. Whilst they still had this ability to see beings, they never felt alone, even if no other human beings were there. The atmosphere of a house or farmstead was made up of this kind of spirituality, which obviously assumed different forms depending on the kind of soul mood in which the work was done. Even nowadays people who are that way inclined, especially children, can still see these 'elemental' beings.

A child with this capacity, who grew up on a farm, often talked about the little folk. After a while the family moved to another farm, and the child was asked if there were little people there as well. 'Yes,' he replied, 'but here they are naked'. There was no woman on this farm. Anyone who understands a bit about pictorial language will realize that despite the farm 'functioning' well from a practical point of view, the child felt that a protective warmth was lacking.

Why do we no longer have little folk?

Let us examine more closely the three stages involved in work: planning; carrying it out (which is usually the lengthy part); and packaging or storing the product, if there is one. People's consciousness is more awake than it was in medieval times, therefore we feel the middle part of a job to be particularly boring and exhausting. Technology came to our aid at the right moment, and wherever it was possible we joyfully delegated this aspect, consisting of the regular repetition of one movement, to machines. This, however, is precisely where the activities of elemental spirits used to be seen.

We can also see the human being in threefold terms, in which the middle or chest part, between the polarities of the head and the limbs, is also rhythmic, and includes the heartbeat and the breathing. Recognizing the parallel, we can say that it is the heart section of our work that has been taken over by technology. It is no wonder we find no satisfaction in what is left!

In the olden days, regular repetition brought spiritual momentum into everyday tasks. Whilst people were hammering stone or threshing corn they felt they were taking part in a sort of universal rhythm. It was especially the lengthy jobs that were done in large groups, either with all the servants or by joining together with their neighbours in, say, the spinning room. This gave communal energy to the work, and people had both company and encouragement. It is well known that people told stories and sang whilst they were spinning. Telling fairy tales and singing are closely related to the rhythmic activities of handicrafts. If you are moving in a regular rhythm it stimulates you to sing or hum. Walking has a similar rhythmic movement, hence the many walking and marching songs.

In our time, as we have seen, songs and stories have succumbed to machines. Machines certainly help to shorten the work, yet they also hinder us from experiencing to the full the quality inherent in a particular job. That is what makes us want to get the job out of the way as quickly as possible so that we can pass on to a more satisfying activity.

My small son, returning one day from visiting a neighbour's boy a little older than himself, reported joyfully:

'Johannes has an electric railway. That is so practical. You can turn it on and then do something else!'

It is worth noticing that it is usually women who, with much patience and tenacity, do the lengthy activities that are still performed by hand. For example, a man will often create the artistic design or template for a hand-woven rug, which a woman executes. Does this happen the other way round? Women seem to have more of a capacity for the rhythmic part of a job and the necessary patience to do it.

When a small boy saw a medieval nativity play he noticed with delight that Mary sang more and Joseph spoke more. 'Singing is more beautiful,' he said, 'and speaking is more important!' This is a rather striking description, perhaps, of a difference between the masculine and the feminine.

Knitting is one of the few rhythmic jobs where women have to a large extent resisted mechanization. This may be connected with the fact that articles made by knitting-machines do not have quite the same quality as hand-knitted items. But women also appreciate having something they can do while they sit and talk to friends. The more perfect a machine, the more it condemns us to loneliness. Modern sewing and knitting-machines are delicate. You need all your concentration, and also have to protect the machine to ensure children do not damage it. Machines invariably make a noise. The farmer out in the fields in his tractor is not lonely only because there is nobody else about. The noise also hinders him from fully experiencing nature, which may be one reason why farmers increasingly suffer from depression.

Children are inventive and frequently hit the nail on the head. I was surprised and highly amused when my two small boys invented the 'song of the vacuum cleaner'. It was a quite specific tune they sang every time the noise of the vacuum cleaner started up. The conquest of technology by song!

Should we therefore condemn 'terrible' technology and do everything by hand again? Certainly not! We may have regrets, and suffer sometimes from attacks of nostalgia, but we can hardly go backwards. Yet there are some things we can do—and the first thing is to start becoming conscious of it. We must be aware of what is happening, not only practically but also psychologically, when we use mechanical appliances. Machines take away the work and help us achieve our purpose with minimum effort. Whilst doing this they also deprive us of the chance to experience *process*. Though we would like to be alive in that area, we remain empty, for there is life only where there is engaged activity. This is why people are never satisfied with the latest model but always want something faster and better.

One should not install a machine just because it exists and is widely advertised, but think it over calmly to decide what is really useful in a specific situation. I once read a priceless story of a man who liked having fresh orange juice every day. So he looked into the choice of fruit-squeezers. He was amazed at the wonders of technical science, and finally chose an apparatus that could squeeze an orange in three seconds. The manufacturers really were true to their word. But what they did not mention is that it took ten minutes to clean the machine afterwards. Our juice drinker eventually returned penitently to grandmother's efficient little hand-squeezer.

Similar surprises often occur. Even a dishwasher is only worthwhile for fairly large families. And even then you should take the social aspect into consideration. Think of all the important conversations that have taken place as people wash up together! The result is not the only thing that matters; it is also the attention people give to such work. To consider this aspect, and to make our choice, is part of our human freedom. A machine not only emancipates us but also puts pressure on us. We feel we ought to use a machine, a car, a computer, because they are there, and other people use them.

It is one of our particularly human duties to control technology and not be controlled by *it*:

All that we have acquired
is threatened by machines
if they presume to rule our spirit
rather than being subservient

(Rainer Maria Rilke)

The attitude you have when you use a machine makes a difference. It should never lose its tool-character by making us dependent upon it, either in a practical or a psychological way. As a tool, though, we should have full respect for it and take it seriously.

The task of acquiring conscious control over machines is particularly one for women, since men are generally more susceptible to the fascination of technical apparatus. One can observe as a mother that masculine assistance is readily offered when it comes to inventing ways of avoiding work. Men are also more likely to be willing to use a machine than do a job by hand.

In Max Frisch's novel *Homo Faber*, the chief male character notes down the following words:

Discussion with Hanna!—regarding technology which (according to her) is the knack of dealing with the world in such a way that we do not have to experience it.

Technicians have the urge to make Creation profitable because they cannot bear to have it as a partner, and do not know what else to do with it; technology is the knack of getting rid of the world because it is too much of an obstacle, e.g. by speeding things up to the point where the world is so diluted that we do not have to experience it. (What Hanna means by this I do not know.)

We cannot turn back evolution and conjure a world without technology. But we can work therapeutically if, by free choice, we persevere at doing certain things at a human tempo, and fill them with human experience—such as knitting a sweater, building a doll's house for the children, or preparing an especially attractive meal. This also provides an opportunity for trying out and practising capacities that we would not otherwise develop because they are not demanded of us. You do not need to be a good cook to warm up a ready-made meal. Modern cookery books are not demanding. They are so 'foolproof' that even the decorative garnish is prescribed. An old cookery book from the 1920s merely tells you, after enumerating the ingredients, to 'knead a good dough with the right amount of flour'. In those days they obviously assumed that a housewife knew what 'the right amount of flour' and a 'good dough' was.

How would it be if homemakers simply refused to have pre-mixed or fast-food meals? This would be the most effective way of combating a frequently indifferent attitude to cooking. But what would we actually be up against? We would probably have to face up to our own indifference, since many of us have lost interest in the creative and artistic process of food preparation.[68]

From our children, though, we could learn how to change

our attitude to things and to live more 'slowly' again, which means being fully alive in the moment. We could also see it as part of their education to teach our children how to do the basic things such as cooking, baking, washing, weaving and spinning. All the old crafts are prototypes which human beings need as soul nourishment in order to feel at home in the world. They are allegorical as well as material processes, which were after all the basis for mechanization, though this is no longer detectable. The process that is open to view in the hand-weaving loom is integrated into and concealed in the weaving machine. The washing moving about in the soapsuds is concealed by the metal walls of the washing machine, visible in most cases only through a small glass window.

Of course it is not just a matter of showing our children old crafts in a rural crafts museum. Increasingly there are good environmental reasons for doing things by hand, and without using strong cleaning agents. Growing your own vegetables, home baking and cooking, in which children often love to be involved, are also good ways to avoid unwanted additives. Modern environmental awareness such as recycling also has a moral dimension for children: they see that something is going to be re-used rather than simply thrown away. And the extra effort of walking or cycling rather than getting in a car likewise promotes healthy will activity.

A homemaker's self-confidence can be boosted by knowing that as a consumer she is an important factor in the economy. It can be satisfying to consciously follow up where the goods you buy come from and how they have been produced or handled. This can help build up a new network of relationships between producers and consumers which connect human beings in an absolutely down-to-earth way.

To conclude, there is one more attribute to be mentioned that belongs to the vocation of a homemaker: arranging your time as you see fit! This certainly does not happen by itself, but demands self-discipline. If you can create a little 'space' between yourself and your work, so that you don't always feel driven by compulsion, a greater sense of ease and enjoyment can arise—a feeling of freedom and self-determination.

It is sometimes difficult to detach oneself, for in a household there is always something to do. In her book *Feminine Mystique,* Betty Friedan includes a chapter called 'Housework Can Be Stretched Like Elastic', where she cites the example of two mothers, each living in nuclear family homes, and each with three children of school age. One was just a 'housewife', the other was a freelance illustrator of books, and their incomes were roughly the same. Both women were busy all day, and the children did not seem neglected in any way. The 'housewife only' one, however, could not even find time in the evening to read something for her own pleasure, whilst the career wife played in a string quartet and pursued her own interests. Such observations are certainly not exaggerated, or only very slightly. Having a job we enjoy can give us the impetus to organize everything else far more easily.

But is that the only incentive? The chance to organize our time in freedom surely offers many additional opportunities—such as, perhaps, establishing a new relationship with nature by sensing the qualities of different times of the day and filling them with appropriate activities. Such things give us a sense of involvement and creativity.

Farmers and gardeners are probably the only people in a similar position. Even just noticing that the sun shines in through the east window in the morning, the south window at midday and the west window in the evening, and produces quite a different atmosphere in each case, contributes towards experiencing the home as a personality with a thoroughly individual character. How different this personality seems when it is raining! Houses facing west and houses facing east affect the life of their occupiers in rather different ways. A young woman—a conscientious housewife and the mother of several children—was seen to go for a rambling walk with her children every morning. According to her, her work went much better if she had been out and seen what kind of day was coming first.

If we consciously try to do particular jobs during the right part of the day we may notice that some things go better in the mornings and others better in the evenings, some better in summer and others better in winter. We cannot observe this if we work in an office or a shop, whereas we can at home. When we bring freedom into such observations, we acquire respect for the dignity and inexorability with which the hours and the seasons take their course, and feel connected with a wider environment. Such awareness safeguards us from losing ourselves in trivialities. Perhaps that is what nature is really asking of us.

Can a Mother Realize her Potential?

Those who see only themselves
can give no light

Lao Tzu

Many women today are deeply absorbed by the intriguing word 'self-actualization'. It is not always quite clear what people understand by this. It often appears to be something that can only be pursued by having a career. What does it actually mean?

The word was coined by the American psychologist Abraham Maslow (1908–70) who researched the motives for human action. He distinguished between actions that serve to satisfy a need—for food, respect, love, etc.—and those we do to develop ourselves in some way. He called the latter self-actualization. He found that people are healthy only if they strive for self-actualization, i.e. if they develop their potential capacities. This is based on the assumption that we may have a way of life in which we cannot fully develop as human beings. If it really were true that motherhood makes our development stagnate, there would be no doubt about the need for resisting it.

Let us turn to some accounts by a few young mothers after the birth of their first child. These come from a booklet entitled 'Women talk about having children':[69]

Gertrud: I believe now that this pregnancy represented a choice between easy-going light heartedness and constant oppressive responsibility. There was only black and white. I could not imagine myself as a mother. Perhaps something I had experienced in my own mother? Being in no position to see or guess at the beautiful and fulfilling side of it, I thought I had to say goodbye to my relatively free existence.

In the first few weeks I just did not want to accept the fact that a baby initially meant restrictions. I was set on having everything as perfectly under control as before. For sheer fear that being a housewife would make me stupid I started buying newspapers every day to keep up with world events. To re-establish contact with the outside world I engaged in activities which brought me slowly but surely to the limits of my strength. I felt shut in and isolated; I could find no identity as a housewife and mother, and thought everything was awful.

Annette: In retrospect I would like to reiterate that having a child makes absolutely everything go off the rails. What with the strain of the birth, the many uncertainties of the new responsibility, physical exhaustion and the constant demands made by a newborn baby all round the clock, I was scarcely able to apply myself to anything else. The household was uncared for, and sex and partnership was a write-off for a long time. I was plagued by poor concentration, difficulties in coming to grips with things, and constant stress. I did not get over my personal low until I had weaned my child and returned to my job. I had a new interest again that was a challenge, and my strength suddenly returned.

Brigitte: In my case I was overwhelmed with a feeling of dependence. I did not feel I was a person any more but 'only' a mother and housewife, existing entirely for the family. What frustrates me so much is the fact that I no longer even get to *do* anything nice, such as knitting or reading a book, or something like that. Nor do I have any time or peace to think a single idea through to the end that might for once have nothing to do with my son. He takes my whole energy and concentration. And I often feel that the responsibility of having my mind on him the whole time is going to crush me.

Even though one knows for certain that women who have borne more than one child speak differently—handling babies is an acquired skill just like anything else—it is clear from such comments how burdensome it is for a modern young woman to readjust to motherhood. It is no longer felt as something natural, to which we accommodate ourselves as a matter of course. The difficulties involved lie in several directions. First of all there are the excessive physical demands that can bring you to the end of your tether. Then you are so tied down and isolated or, even worse, afraid of being tied down and isolated. Lastly there is the lack of mental challenge, and the feeling of losing yourself in impersonal activities without really finding your identity as a mother. So the problems are partly of a practical and social nature, and partly psychological.

No doubt the role of motherhood came more easily to women in former times, when they were less intellectual. Let us see what Anna Magdalena Bach, the second wife of Johann Sebastian Bach, and a gifted singer, has to say about the beginning of her marriage. Bach already had four children from his first marriage.

A.M.B. When we got married in 1721, Friedeman was eleven, Emanuel seven, little Johann Gottfried six and dear

Katherine two years older than Friedeman. So right from the beginning I had a little family to look after and mother. No doubt in imitation of their father's kind example, the little ones loved me immediately with their whole hearts and initiated me into their joys and sorrows.

Soon afterwards an even greater happiness came to me. I was given a child. I was expecting my firstborn—something that surely no woman ever forgets. The point arrived when the baby clothes were hanging by the fire to warm, and the good old midwife brought Sebastian in to me once more. He looked a little anxious, however he said cheerfully: 'My pet, all the Bach women have had their children happily.' Then his voice changed suddenly, and putting his arm round me he whispered: 'Poor lamb, how it hurts me that you will have to suffer pain!' And these words, and the loving sound of his voice, comforted me until our firstborn was safely delivered. We had altogether 13 children. God's blessing was with us, and He made me as fertile as the vine on the wall of my husband's house.[70]

Feminists might see these words as the expression of appalling subservience to a patriarch. But even if they are not an illustration of the female search for identity they are a testimony of tremendous inner harmony and psychological health. In those days the inner attitude with which a woman accepted motherhood, as well as the whole social situation of a young mother, must have been very different.

In earlier times not just mothers but *everyone* was far more firmly rooted in the place they lived in. Consequently they did not experience motherhood so much as a shackle limiting their freedom. Whoever would have wanted to rush off to Italy or Israel for a holiday? What wife would have wanted to get a degree or an office job? Fundamentally speaking it is men's greater freedom of movement that generates in women, in our civilization, the feeling of dependence and subordination.

Formerly a girl passed from the restricting nature of the parental home into the relatively greater freedom of her own family, whereas today she usually leaves the greater freedom of a profession or professional training for the lesser freedom of family life. No wonder that for many women this is a shock. A student who is used to a life of unrestricted friendships with her fellow students suddenly finds herself hemmed in by often very cramped living conditions and a great deal of practical work. She does not see why it should all land on her alone, and thus we now see the welcome fact that fathers share more than before in looking after the children. Fathers gain from this, of course, as it also redresses the imbalance created otherwise by too one-sided specialism in their lives. As long ago as 1905, Rosa Mayreder wrote:[71]

> Motherhood is a guarantee that a woman's mind will not be plunged into the same kind of incongruous relationship with natural and primitive areas of existence as is the intellect of men who do brain work.

Practical work ensures that our sound common sense remains intact, that we stay in touch with the real world. If a woman's thinking is often more practical than a man's, that is surely because she almost always engages more immediately with real life. This really should not be viewed negatively. It becomes a problem only when a woman who also has other aims in life finds herself compelled to give all her energy to mundane tasks. Looking after a child allows for very little free time. In addition, the household suddenly requires more effort: cooking and washing for the child, cleaning and tidying up. A woman with cultural interests is bound to feel these restraints as painful renunciation. The amount of self-lessness and devotion that are needed are not simply a given but have to be acquired, which can be hard work. In addition to this—and this is the psychological side of the matter—one often simply does not feel motivated, and cannot find one's 'mother identity'.

Why is this? 'Perhaps something I had experienced in my own mother?' These are sad times if daughters see in their mother's example more of a deterrent than a model. In that case it is no wonder that motherhood does not become a joyful goal worth striving for. Obviously that kind of mother did not succeed in developing her personality through motherhood, i.e. pursuing 'self-actualization'.

Self-actualization means developing our individual potential. Do we know exactly what this is when we are young? Are we sure which direction our development should take? In fact we can never 'actualize' all our potential. If they examine themselves honestly, most mothers, even the emancipated ones, must admit that they owe their children a great many of the qualities and traits that appear in their personality. Women who have no children may actually, in a quite different way, be deprived of an important experience and lack something that life can bring to a woman. After all, the development of our personality involves the fact that we inhabit a female body.[72]

It can give us food for thought to see that women who died young and who, before their death, looked back over their lives, ranked motherhood very highly as the fulfilment of female existence and therefore of their human development.[73]

Evidently this fulfilment no longer comes of itself through the biological fact of becoming a mother.

It is much more a matter of integrating motherhood into our own personality. This means, however, accepting all its different stages and aspects and seeing the positive side of anything unpleasant that occurs. A mother who succeeds in doing this will have gained a lot as a human being. She will be enriched by many good and also amusing experiences and will acquire maturity from the challenge of staying calm in the face of difficulties. To do the same supposedly insignificant, homely activities again and again, year in and year out, strengthens will and deepens feelings. A rhythm is established which lives in us, and to subtler observation it becomes clear that these mundane tasks involve real engagement with the world.

Doubtless there are many vocations in which there is more opportunity for self-awareness and self-assertion than in a mother's domestic chores. Yet motherhood is not a serious hindrance to developing our personality. The kind of self-awareness that depends on a job outside the home and other people's recognition is weaker than the kind that results from perhaps unacknowledged self-discipline and regular practical work. We women are in danger of constantly aspiring to outward independence whilst remaining inwardly weak and dependent. The greatest obstacle to development is the belief that it is the circumstances in which we find ourselves in life that stand in the way of self-actualization.

Of course this is not to deny real difficulties of both an outer and inner kind. For instance, being alone so much can make us unsociable, and really weaker for sheer lack of a challenge; and we should do something about it in good time. A trip to the theatre, an outing, walk or even a longer journey—whatever is possible in the particular situation—is often helpful.

There is also a little trick to help people overcome a sense of inferiority or insignificance. Self-praise is not normally a virtue, but if you are in the habit of being hard on yourself about all sorts of minor things, it can work wonders to praise yourself a little instead, on the quiet: 'That was a lovely dinner I made!', 'It's amazing that I got through today so calmly when the children are ill!', 'I would never have dreamed I could sew this well!', 'A good thing I got all the laundry done!' and so on. This may seem very silly, but it can give a little uplift in a wearisome routine, and remind us that our work is actually important, even if people hardly notice it.

It is also helpful if you can talk regularly with other people in the same situation, for you can always do with new motivation. And I don't just mean bumping into your neighbour in the street and hearing what she gave her child for bronchitis. Something more like a regular study evening is good, where you work with others, possibly on an educational or child-rearing theme. Not only can this be fun, but it can also provide a stimulus and a sense of being in it together, even if you are often actually alone.

Working on a quite different, unrelated theme can be just as important, enabling us, on a regular basis, to gain that vital inner distance and have the opportunity to look at things from a higher vantage point. Regular churchgoing in past times used to bring a great deal of meaning into daily life. We are in urgent need of something similar today, as well as the chance to withdraw every day for a little while to reflect or cultivate our inner life. It is often extremely difficult for a mother to find the time for a prayer or a meditation, let alone a room where she will not be disturbed. However, if it can be arranged, this is a source of strength which is increasingly vital in the modern world. Some mothers manage to get up ten minutes before the children do, and use this time for their inner work. For others a later time during the morning is better. The evening review of the day also has its place. If you let the day's experiences flow past in reverse order as though watching your life from without, and without assessing or judging them, you can find how many difficulties gradually and naturally resolve themselves. This is another and very effective way of gaining some objective distance from what happens in your life, and at the same time acts as stimulus for the next day. It enables you to let go of problems and also to enter sleep with calm and hopefulness.[74]

Doing all these things helps avoid a danger that is even worse than being discontented or unsociable, because you do not so readily notice that something is wrong: I mean that your horizon is restricted. There are mothers who have a circle of interests that scarcely reaches beyond the washing machine, dinner and a clean house. You only get into this sort of stagnation, of course, if you think motherhood only really involves getting the family washed and fed. As soon as you participate in children's emotional and mental development you get caught up in their progress—in which you will constantly find new challenges and be confronted by new things.

If you have an occasional quiet afternoon to yourself it is worth taking stock and asking yourself what you have learnt from motherhood. You may realize, perhaps, that you have become stronger and more independent through having taken on this responsibility, that you are no longer, for instance, as hesitant as you were, and that you have got a better grip on your moodiness. There may even be positive physical changes: mothers get ill less often because they cannot afford to be; they are no longer carsick because their children suffer from it, etc. Motherhood gives us stamina, makes us hard working, persevering, attentive, unselfish and self-sacrificing. The list is fairly endless, though of course our failings and acknowledgement of them are also equally part of the experience.

Up to now we have spoken of the opportunities which motherhood gives us to develop our own personality. These can of course only be tapped to the full if we have the will to identify fully with motherhood. Over and above this we can strive to draw on our personal interests and abilities to enrich family life. A woman who had been to art school before she became a mother put all her creative ability, which she initially had to shelve, into creating beautiful celebrations for her children's birthdays. She also painted picture books for them, made toys and embroidered their clothes. Another mother, trained in tailoring, made clothes for the whole family. A horticulturalist particularly enjoyed growing flowers and vegetables. Even an interest in literature can be put to work by telling[75] fairy tales to young children, and adventure stories to the bigger ones. And later on you can read them more challenging poetical works. There are epics such as the *Iliad* and the *Odyssey*, *Parzival* and the Finnish epic the *Kalevala* that really lend themselves much better to reading aloud. As was the case in the old communities where such stories circulated, their rhythmic beauty can enliven and bind the family community more closely together. You can of course also choose lighter and more humorous reading, alternating this with more serious tales. Listening to stories read aloud has a social element about it, and sows the seeds for a love of literature. It can also be wonderfully creative to make up your own stories in response to the children and your perception of their needs, or to create stories with a healing effect if there has been an upset of some kind.[76]

I could give many more examples. The main obstacle to self-actualization—to repeat myself—is believing your circumstances prevent it, for this belief itself hinders you from doing what you can do with your whole heart, and thus make real.

The more you develop and cultivate interests of your own whilst the children are growing up the easier it will be, when they are bigger, for you to let them go. Some mothers cannot let their children go because they still need them to justify their own existence. That is the wrong kind of self-actualization as a mother, which ends up being a kind of reverse dependency of the parent on the child. When children are bigger it is not only possible but helpful for both mother and children if the mother has a part-time job, for letting go is not at all easy if you have previously fully identified yourself with motherhood.

Although we won't of course become indifferent all of a sudden but accompany with loving interest all that our children do, we should nevertheless stand back and watch them from a distance while they learn from experience. The following sentiment by Rilke certainly applies here:[77]

> Loving someone, there's one option only:
> to let go, for to hold them fast is easy
> and needs no prior learning.

At no other age are children so sensitive to being watched over as they are at puberty. They want to be free to come and go, and to creep into the house and out of it, even if they have nothing to hide. So it is a good thing at this time if we have interests other than checking on the youngsters all the time to see what time they come home in the evening. We must get them to feel that although this is not a matter of indifference to us we do trust them, and grant them more and more space in which to be responsible for themselves.[78]

It may sound as though a teenager does not need any more bringing up. This is not the case, yet such education now consists almost entirely in the self-education of the parents. Youngsters certainly keep an eye on how their parents behave, even if they don't always seem to do so.

It is particularly painful for children to have to experience marriage crises whilst they are in puberty, as this is the time when the ground is prepared for the way they will behave later on towards the opposite sex. Their awakening soul life is extremely fragile and sensitive, and in their deepest inner life they seek an ideal example.

We shall have to deny ourselves certain things for the sake of our children. For example, there is no point in forbidding them to smoke if Dad is a chain smoker, or if clouds of smoke billow from the school staff room.

We may discover one of our children has some undesirable qualities we also have, but we now see them mirrored to us and no longer mitigated by the charms of childhood. A hot-tempered mother may notice that her daughter has the same tendency. Then she will have to say to herself: 'We cannot live together like this, we'll constantly be at each others' throats. I am the older one, so it is up to me to stop being like this.'

It is very hard if you have made every effort to set your child a good example and then witness youngsters develop-ing qualities and doing things that are absolutely foreign to their parents, and also doing themselves harm into the bargain. There can be cases, such as drug addiction, that may be regarded as an illness, where strong intervention in some form may be called for. With understanding and restraint, however, one can usually avoid the worst excesses of adolescence. Back in the nineteenth century, Therese Schröer gave sensible advice which, however antiquated its language now, still remains valid today. In her book 'Practical education for the young',[79] she writes:

> The young have periods of transition, and this is where forbearance and gentle guidance are needed. They often resemble sleepwalkers on a narrow and dangerous path. So what is the use of angry shouting? All we can allow ourselves is to make suggestions, for they can neither be pushed nor hurried over the threshold from one phase of life to another. We must watch over them and accompany them with peace, love and self-denial. If we imagine we have grown too weary and have completely lost heart, we should remind ourselves: Tomorrow, with God's help, it could be different! And very often it is. In a matter of hours or days our daughter or our son will have shed their chrysalis, and their newly awakened soul will spread its young wings and fly to meet us.

We must never believe that our own inner attitude has no effect. In one case a mother wrote to her son: 'I know that you are going through great difficulties. But you have coped with trouble before. I believe you are strong enough to cope with this.' The answer she received was: 'If you think so, then I can.'

All the faculties a mother developed for mothering and educating her children when they were small have to be laid aside when they grow up, and it is now a matter of taking a sincere and open interest in every surprise they confront her with, maintaining her belief in the possibility of a positive outcome. In other words, a really open mind and genuine interest goes a long way in sustaining the relationship.

Just as we have the chance to become a child all over again with our own children, so we can become an adolescent again with our own adolescents, not by denying our true age but by sharing in the many interests youngsters and their friends bring into the house. After puberty it is quite obvious that we suddenly have growing individualities before us, for whom the fact that they are related to us is very much of secondary importance. Some children may of course share more in their mother's interests, and some more in those of their father. But interests can also crop up which have never existed in the family before. In any case there is an opportunity for discussion and dialogue. Life can be inwardly enriched and grow suddenly multi-hued, as our children grow unawares into our friends.

A mother who herself keeps changing and developing will not be a discouraging example to her children. In fact, sometimes a daughter writes the kind of letter to her mother that Anne Morrow Lindbergh did shortly after her marriage:[80]

New York City (beginning of May 1929)

Dearest Mother,
I have been sitting here thinking, and thinking about you. And I cannot find the right words. I should like to tell you that you're really great. Most of the time I sit apathetically and egoistically at the margins of your full and wonderful life and seem to take you for granted. But one is rather

overwhelmed and inclined to forget it or not to realize it, for you yourself never seem to realize that you are wonderful! And so I thought I would tell you for once what everyone should have been continually telling you— what everybody says about you, but that you never hear: that you are simply a wonderful person, a rare, lovely, astonishingly alive person, receptive and open to everything.

That is the highest form of lifestyle. This has dawned on me more and more. I knew it instinctively as our interests widened. It was astonishing, for at each phase we went through, and in each area we discovered—each new enthusiasm—you were there, entering into everything with warm understanding, just as though you yourself had also only just discovered it. But that is what you are like with everybody and in a thousand and one subjects. The trouble is that nobody can appreciate it to the full; nobody is big enough to realize it fully!

What is our Calling?

You are not free if you can do what you want
but, rather, if you can become what you should.

Paul de Lagarde

Motherhood is a great, important task. Yet in our time historical necessity dictates that women embark on professional careers. This brings us to the fundamental question of the significance of a person's work in their biography—a significance which has changed over the centuries, and even from decade to decade.

The word 'job' entered the vocabulary of Central Europe on the wave of Americanism following the Second World War. As a foreign word in the German language it acquired a meaning slightly different from the original English one. What we understand by it here is 'casual work for the purpose of earning money'. If we want to make a major purchase, or we are planning to go on a world tour, we have first of all to do a job for a while. So the word is connected with the purely material aspect of work and its remuneration. A 'job' often requires little or no preliminary training. Workers are easily replaced. This entails the highest measure of freedom in the sense of lack of commitment both for the employer and for the employee.

Something different from this is implied by working in a profession. As a young person we look for the right vocation, i.e. we choose an activity we believe will satisfy us over a long period, and pursue a vocational training. The longer the training the more valuable we are as a specialist, and cannot so easily be replaced by someone else. Thus we do not only earn money but also acquire status and recognition. Participating in public life with the success and the financial independence this entails strengthens our self-confidence. The women of our century are aware of needing this kind of boost. This is why they want to go into a career in the 'outside world', even if financial reasons do not absolutely necessitate this. After having obediently submitted for centuries to the role life allotted them, they now want to be free to choose what they do.

We do not notice quite so readily that it is only in fairly recent times that men, too, have had the chance to choose their own profession—which means finding their identity as an individual. In the Middle Ages a man's profession was determined almost entirely by his family and social milieu: for instance the eldest son became a farmer and the youngest a monk, whether this satisfied their souls or not.

The instances that most fully embody 'self-actualization' in any era are those of inspired human beings who were exceptions both within their own families and to the time in which they lived. These are the ones who feel 'called' to do something. They often develop tremendous strength to realize their impulses against all odds. They no doubt feel they would be denying their own innate being if they were not to do so. In fact most of them feel they are doing their work in the service of a higher power. We could enumerate many examples, such as Joan of Arc or Beethoven, van Gogh or Marie Curie. People like this are interested neither in profit, success nor recognition, which mostly does not come to them anyway until after their death. They look at their work entirely from the ideal aspect.

Ordinary professional life takes place somewhere between the material and the ideal extremes—between a 'job' and a 'calling'. For some people it tends more in one direction, and with others more in the other. Achieving a perfect balance is rare. A 'job' is connected with the non-individual aspect of a person, and a vocation with the individuality. While we can speak of job-sharing, a vocation is essentially indivisible.

For some people their profession remains just a job all their lives. Since factory work was introduced in the nineteenth century, the professions have to a great extent moved towards the material end of the spectrum. This gives more and more significance to the difference between work and free time.

As a person's work is usually away from home there is a strict division between public life and private life. Private life is a person's personal sphere, and it is indiscreet for others, unless invited, to take too great an interest in it. One could say that the dualism which once underpinned a whole philosophical outlook has nowadays become a way of life. From a positive perspective this gives us a chance to withdraw and to protect our personality. The right to have 'a room of one's own' is an important factor for us Europeans.[81] More negatively, our public and our private life can be in contradiction with each other. This often starts with spare-time idealists who have the funds to pursue other concerns. It also includes the sort of people who, as teachers and lecturers, propagate fine, moral thoughts, but whose private life does not match up to this. It is possible to work as a scientist on weekdays and cultivate a totally different kind of thinking in church on Sundays, or to be a chemist who produces insecticides and chemical fertilizers, and in his spare time supports environmental protection.

However, a person who lives his real life in his spare time

but pursues a different profession solely to earn money is not bound to be a schizophrenic in the accepted sense of the word, nor even a materialist. One can feel 'called' to do something but simply not be able to put it into a form that is paid for.

When young people choose a vocation they will usually, of course, look for one that both covers their basic needs and which they will enjoy doing: in other words, a profession that matches their interests and abilities. This kind of vocation is getting more and more difficult to find. Real callings are rare; many people are good all-rounders yet only moderately gifted in any direction. This often makes it very difficult to make a career decision.

However, the very existence in our civilization of this opportunity to make a personal choice and decision about our vocation is connected with humanity's advancing individualization, as we have already pointed out. It is an act of freedom. This is why from the very beginning the battle for an equal chance to be educated and to enter the professions has played such a large part in the women's movement.

This battle has not yet been fought to the finish. Yet it is pretty well taken for granted nowadays that a girl trains for a vocation instead of staying at home and waiting for a husband, as used to happen among the middle classes in centuries gone by. And it does not happen very often either that a girl goes to university only for the purpose of angling for a husband so that she can return to domesticity. It is far more often the case that a girl wants to continue with her education or her vocation as well as being in a relationship. But it is only natural that in due course the desire arises to have a child, or that without much pre-planning a child simply arrives.

This produces a dilemma: women's conflict between motherhood and a vocation.

The following words by Rosa Mayreder were first published back in 1905:[82]

> We can certainly say that women constitute the child-bearing half of humanity; but in the very statement that a woman's vocation is motherhood, you overstep the proper boundaries of generalization by introducing the concept of a vocation which permits no separate individualization.

In other words, a woman's tasks as a mother and an individual cannot easily be combined. In the previous chapter we endeavoured to present an approach to integrating a woman's general tasks into personal development. We shall now look at it from the opposite point of view.

It is only too understandable that many women do not want to be pushed automatically into 'vocational' motherhood that they have not chosen for themselves, and which they do not see as their sole task in life, simply because they would like to have children.

In order to solve this problem people search for alternative, unconventional modes of life. Unfortunately there is no generally valid solution. Just as in previous times people looked to the older generation for an example, nowadays they turn to their peers or to those who are scarcely older than they and who are basically just as helpless. Social changes can help only to the extent that they bring about a loosening of the old structures and create space for individual efforts. This suggests that we should look for a possible way of combining both 'vocations'—both motherhood and a profession. Yet now that our world has become so mechanized, and working environments so unsuitable for children, there

are ever fewer activities that can be done in their presence
except crafts and gardening. Almost all vocations require us to
have our children looked after elsewhere. But how do we do
this? The demand for more childcare (crèche, kindergarten,
etc.) is loud, but often its most enthusiastic proponents are
either childless women (e.g. Simone de Beauvoir) or
governments that wish to see mothers returning to work as
soon as possible. Mothers know what it means to have to take
a child from home every single day, even if he or she cries or
has a cold. It can also be difficult to miss witnessing important
steps in your child's development.

In socialist countries the family was indeed partly dissolved
as social unit, with state educational and childcare provision
giving woman greater freedom to have a career. This is of
course not entirely unrealistic in an age of divorce and the
breakdown of family life. But in those countries people could
tell a story or two about just how difficult it was to organize
all these public institutions, how long the waiting lists were,
and in what a routine way the children were dealt with, for
there was no personal interest behind it. A young mother
from the former East Germany tells us how she felt when she
finally got a place in a crèche for her child who was barely
one:[83]

> I accepted the fact with a mixture of laughter and tears.
> What was I to do? To be honest, I should have dearly
> loved to stay at home. If only I had! I remember those days
> with horror. Tears every day, constant illness (colds,
> diarrhoea, vomiting . . .). What ought I to be doing? Thank
> goodness Granny can fetch the children at 2 o'clock!

Many young women would really like to do full justice to
motherhood and yet be able, if possible, to work on their

personal interests, within certain limits. They wish that the value of what they are doing were a little more appreciated generally. Here are quotes from several young mothers:

Bettina: If it is not even acknowledged that through her work of looking after her home and bringing up her children a woman is working constructively for society at both an emotional and physical level, then when she becomes pregnant she is driven into a passive corner . . . Yet women do not give up their personality and individuality as soon as they become pregnant. 'The child and my pregnancy belong to my development as a person. They are part of life, but they are not the whole of life, not the whole explanation. There would always be something missing.' I noted this down in my diary during my pregnancy.

Gabriele: Sometimes I felt isolated and far removed from the rest of the world. All my former acquaintances who had no children could not see why I had no time any more, that I was often too tired to go out in the evenings and was often unable even to phone them. They increasingly withdrew from me. This is compounded by the fact that this is not a child-loving country: dogs have more rights than children. You have to make sure your child does not make a sound when you take her out, go shopping with her or visit a restaurant. All this sort of thing becomes a problem. Women with children do not fit in or belong to our modern society; they are pushed off into playgrounds; they belong in the home, and your work with your children is not acknowledged.

Doris: Again and again I meet with indifference and lack of understanding from former friends. What really surprises me is that the more dedicated a women's libber a woman is, the less interested she is in my new circumstances. Is it insecurity or fear that prevents them from dealing with this pressing problem?

We have ascertained that the vocation of a mother in many ways does not fit into our pattern of vocations. So the general conclusion is therefore that it is not a vocation. However, we can put the question another way. Is there possibly something wrong with our picture of vocations? Is our idea of vocational work the only possible and right one for human development? Is the vocation of a mother simply outdated or, perhaps—because it has not yet been overspecialized—does it have the very qualities lacking in other professions that can be seeds for the future?

Let us take another look at the problem young people face today in choosing a vocation. People waver between, say, being a craftsperson or a university professor, a programmer or a nurse. The young are then sent to a career advisor to test their potential. I know of no single case where a career advisor gave really useful advice. Young people often have to change their vocations several times before they find the right one.

It is amazing that Rudolf Steiner already pointed to this problem as early as 1916, long before it had come to general attention.[84]

What is still possible in many instances today—though only as a vestige of past times that people cling to out of habit—will soon prove to be nothing more than empty talk, the sort of high-sounding phrases that are still held in such great esteem today: for instance, that we should observe children and let them develop their innate capacities. This particular phrase will soon prove to be an empty cliché. For people will soon see that children born from now on will show signs of their previous incarnations in a much more complicated way than was the case in the fourth post-Atlantean epoch (about 800 BC–AD 1400). People will be far more complex in nature than could possibly have been imagined in earlier times, when things were far simpler. Those who consider themselves particularly good at discovering what particular career is suitable for each adolescent may have to realize that all this is nothing but wild speculation.

But apart from all this, in the relatively near future life will become so complex that the word 'vocation' will take on an entirely different meaning. Nowadays we often still think of a vocation as being connected with our inner life, whereas most people's profession has in fact nothing inward about it. We picture a vocation as something a person is called to do by virtue of their innate qualities. However, if we question people objectively about this, especially in the cities, how many of them do you think would say, 'I am in my particular profession because I am convinced this is the only one that matches the abilities and inclinations I have had all my life?' Very few city people would say that; and your experience would not lead you to believe them if they did. To an ever-increasing extent a profession is the kind of thing a person is called to do by objective circumstances in the world. What nowadays calls on or requires our work is outside not within us: the organization or the network, or the machine if you like— it really does not matter what name you give it. This will grow increasingly the case and, as a result, what human-kind achieves through professional work will at the same

time become detached from us as individuals and become
more objective.

It increasingly seems that the fear of the vocation of
motherhood is more of a social problem than a personal one.
If a mother's activities qualified as a vocation it would be far
easier to take a positive attitude to it and accept it as part of
personal development.

It would have considerable significance psychologically if a
mother's work was financially recompensed and there were
some kind of motherhood income. As our world unfortunately functions on the basis of 'it's worth nothing if it costs
nothing', this would mean not only greater financial versa-
tility for the housewife but above all greater regard for her.

This is, of course, not an ideal but an admission of existing
circumstances. We should be absolutely clear that a mother's
'productivity' could at the most be paid for only in general
terms. An activity of this kind defies calculation either in
terms of money or time, as it is a matter of qualities that
cannot be grasped quantitatively. The motivation to undertake a job of work always come from our spiritual core: love
for the work and the people, insight into the need for giving
help, etc. This applies fundamentally to all vocations, but
especially to the caring professions; and as long as this is not
acknowledged the crisis situation in which the caring professions find themselves will only get worse. The vocation of
mother is different from public vocations not only as regards
the lack of payment. You cannot give notice, you are tied to
one place and have no set leisure hours. There is a similarity
here with all caring professions. In a care-home one also has a
human connection with the sick, the elderly or children, and
this is damaged if the careworker gives notice. In order to

avoid this, nursing personnel usually work on a rota basis, an extremely questionable solution.

Some young people have realized for themselves that things will need to be different in future. Rather than asking, 'Where do my special gifts lie?' they ask, 'Where am I needed?' They look at what the world requires, and decide, in freedom, to follow where this takes them. Precisely this is likely to give them the greatest satisfaction. They become farmers or helpers in the Third World, and are not primarily interested in the salary or the working hours. That is, they do exactly the same as a young woman does when she becomes a mother and resolves to accept the new situation. She, too, has to say: 'Although motherhood is not an activity in which I can express my abilities particularly well, I am facing one of life's challenges, and I want to do it justice. I choose this vocation for as long as necessary. Afterwards I will pursue something else.' We can see that this starts to resolve the discrepancy between motherhood and vocation.

It would be a good thing if people increasingly adopted the principle of accepting necessity or inevitability in this kind of way, which in no way contradicts personal freedom.

This attitude to our profession or vocation will mean, of course, that we are less emotionally caught up in our work, and can retain a certain distance from it. At the same time it will become important to discover the relationship that exists between what we are doing and the human and natural environment. This will lead to the development of a feeling of responsibility for global relationships that is absolutely indispensable for the future.

The Conflict Between Life and Work

For somewhere an old enmity exists
between life and the great endeavour.

Rainer Maria Rilke

Our aptitudes and innate gifts are becoming more and more complex. This does not exclude the possibility that we might have a special talent in one particular direction. A talent is a task. To put your whole energy into serving the world without regard to your individual capacities and gifts means ultimately to wither in soul. The seeds that lie within us need to grow and mature. This is what Rilke called the 'great endeavour', which can come into conflict with the immediate demands of life.

Hans Sachs was a shoemaker and also a poet, and the same was true of Jakob Boehme. We do not know how these men reconciled these two activities.

If a homemaker feels the need to do intellectual or artistic work—not only as a recreation and a hobby—she soon notices that it is not only a question of having time for it. Intellectual work needs concentration and no interruptions. You have to withdraw into your centre and find the right way to express yourself from within. A mother's work has quite a different orientation. She has to spread her inner forces over her human environment so as to be conscious of everything that concerns the young ones in her care. In this process she forgets herself and finds satisfaction in the joys and successes of others. This is not a contemplative orientation.

Anne Morrow Lindbergh is of the same opinion when she writes in *Gift from the Sea*:

> I gradually realize, with a wistful smile, why saints were so seldom married. I am convinced that, contrary to any previous belief, it has nothing to do with chastity or children. It has primarily to do with dissipation, with the bearing, rearing, feeding and bringing up of children; with the household and its hundred and one demands, with human ties and their many burdens: a woman's normal occupations are usually the opposite of creative life, or of contemplative life and the life of a saint. The problem is not just woman and vocation, woman and family, woman and independence. It goes much deeper than that: How can I remain collected in the midst of life's dissipations? How do I keep my balance despite the centrifugal force that is trying to pull me away from my centre? How do I remain strong in defiance of the knocks that shake me and threaten to damage the cog of my wheel?

Concentrating on oneself and devotion to others are mutually exclusive. You cannot practise them both at once just as little as you can breathe in and out simultaneously. Simultaneity is impossible; but a rhythmic alternation between breathing in and breathing out is a healthy, life-giving process. If we look at this in terms of the various qualities that work involves we have the task of finding the right rhythm. The primary difficulty is always the changeover from one to the other.

Until now this has been mainly a problem for men, and they often fail to achieve it. Men who do intellectual work, particularly, often find it difficult to leave their sphere of work and return fully to the family circle—so that they are not only physically present but are there in full consciousness. The absent-minded philosopher is often a figure of fun. But a mother has to be available for her children not only just half-heartedly but with her whole heart and soul.

Some women can change from one thing to another very quickly. They may have been playing the piano, but the moment they sit down at table with their children they are fully involved in everybody's individuals concerns. Others cannot manage to tear themselves away so quickly from an absorbing activity. A kindergarten teacher gave a report of a child who showed clear signs of being psychologically deprived. His mother worked, but only whilst the boy was in the kindergarten. Then she fetched him home and spent the rest of the day with him. But at home she was obviously still absorbed in her work. When she gave it up the child flourished.

Another woman, in contrast, did not work, but because she did not do so she felt so cramped and cut off from the world that she acquired an inferiority complex. This also had a negative effect on her children. When she took up a career she became happier, and it was a blessing for her whole family.

As a further example, a young woman with three children took up politics because she needed a stimulus. Her husband was in full agreement, and he even reduced his own working hours so that he could spend more time with their children. The wife was so successful that it meant her work increased; but she still aspired to be a good mother as well. Both the partners found that a 'great endeavour' always has the tendency to claim the *whole* of you. And the husband discovered that renouncing a little bit of one's career scarcely works unless you have no interest in it. As the children saw quite a lot of both parents it did not appear as though they suffered at all. But the relationship between the parents became increasingly tense, as they had practically no time left for each other. In the short periods they were together the friction increased until they finally separated. Work thus undermined their relationship.

Some women, knowing of these difficulties, have renounced motherhood right from the start because they feel an intense vocation. One example was the singer Kathleen Ferrier (1912–53), who was very fond of children and therefore did not find this decision easy.[85]

All these examples show how difficult it is to combine work and life, because they are in fact opposites. Life requires one to be social; and work—as self-actualization in a male way—appears to be anti-social. This is not meant in a moral sense. Without an anti-social element we cannot find ourselves, since this inevitably involves gaining some distance from others. It is not always a matter of dramatic clashes. A poet's need for solitude is also anti-social.

Rainer Maria Rilke experienced this anti-social element very deeply and painfully, bound up with the fact of being a poet. His work required of him a lifetime of attentiveness and concentration so that he would not miss the inspired and creative moments. Human relationships, however, need time, cultivation and devotion. These disturb inner concentration, drawing it from the centre to the periphery. Rilke was already tormented by this conflict during the short period when he lived with his wife; he separated from her, but never divorced her. He carried out his obligations to her and their little daughter with complete dedication, maintaining a correspondence with them and supporting them financially according to his circumstances, but he was not able to live with them permanently. Later on he had a few other intimate friendships that could have led to living together, but he extricated himself time and again. In his last years in Valais, Switzerland, he was still oppressed by the problem of having to renounce all human contact because of his work.

Being as I am, any kind of equal human relationship, based on mutual help, would almost inevitably require a degree of human exchange that would immediately risk my having to expend an incalculable amount of soul energy and lead to rivalry with my work. Perhaps it is only in *these* particular years, when I have so much work and reflection to catch up on, that it is such a danger. But I am becoming more and more aware that I must indeed decide between communicating with people and doing my work. It is as though I really have only *one thing left* to give, which can either be communicated directly to a fellow human being or instead be preserved in enduring artistic form, as it were for general use . . .

These things are diverging increasingly, as though there were only a single thing remaining to be communicated in one way or another, when I have made my decision, for it cannot be passed on in two ways. And although, from a higher point of view, it may make no difference whether a person expends his last and most important work in this form or that: in a quiet but enduringly effective word to a friend, or for all to see, in a form that can pass the test of time. Yet my whole disposition and the course of my life pushes me in the direction of the latter form (certainly not out of vanity!) and somehow obliges me to pursue it.[86]

Just as a woman wanting to have a career can feel hesitant about needing a housekeeper—that is, having to pay another woman to work in the home so that she can find 'self-actualization' in the world—Rilke was also dubious about being dependent on the work of servants:

> If I had the strength to isolate myself better I should far prefer to be helped by one of my equals than by someone in service (which is such an ambiguous situation under present conditions; and more or less an excuse, since social enlightenment has suppressed the natural instinct and innocence which caused people to believe that 'service' is just as flourishing and rewarding a way of life as any other, provided it is done with a cheerful heart).

Rilke regarded it as an agonizing riddle that it is nearly always women who serve in this way, spend all their energy doing it and, in so doing, cut themselves off from the possibility of a 'great endeavour'.

No doubt this was partly what gave him such a shock when the highly gifted young artist Paula Modersohn-Becker died in childbirth. He felt it was unjustified that all the potential available to her as an artist succumbed to the general lot of womanhood. This is why this death grew for him into something more than the death of an individual and became a symbolic event. The requiem he wrote for her is one of the most profound expositions of a woman's conflict between motherhood and a career:[87]

> How brief was your life, if set against
> those hours when you sat and drew
> the many forces of your diverse future
> silently down to infuse the child
> growing in the womb—who was
> also destiny. O woe, our work.

O work beyond all strength. You did it
day after day, dragged yourself to it
and threaded the lovely weft upon the loom
and plied all threads of yours a different way.
And still, in the end, had courage to celebrate.

. . .

And so you died, as women used to do,
the old-fashioned way in the sheltering house:
a childbirth death, of a woman who tries
to close herself again but can't;
for all the darkness that she also bears
returns and urgently rushes in.

The poet then calls for an angel to carry the lament and plaint
to God:

For far too long this suffering has gone on,
and none can bear it: it's too hard for us
this muddled suffering of mistaken love
which building on assuaging time and habit
calls itself rightful but springs from injustice.
Which man can say possession is his right?

For Rilke it was an absolutely real experience that this young
woman, called away to another realm of existence so
unexpectedly, could not be dead like other dead souls, but
that she had returned and appeared to be imploring. Was she
drawn back because her life had not yet been completed?
Neither the path of life nor the path of work had been fulfilled. She had begun on both: the path of an artist and the
path of motherhood, and death had cut off both beginnings.

One can sense an even greater tragedy in the life of

Camille Claudel (1864–1943), sister of the poet Paul Claudel.[88] As a young, highly gifted sculptress she became a pupil of Auguste Rodin when he was already at the height of his artistic powers. Their relationship developed into a very close working partnership. She had a considerable share in a number of Rodin's works (e.g. the *Citizens of Calais*). Her own gifts, however, were completely dominated and monopolized by his.

Through working together an intimate love relationship also sprang up between them—for Camille the great passion of her life, but for Rodin it was one among others. He had lived for many years with a woman who looked after him with great devotion, and he was not prepared to give her up in favour of Camille. Camille was expecting a child, but she did not keep it full term. She left Rodin and tried to go her own way as an artist. She certainly found recognition, but inwardly she could not bear to be separated from him. Thus she was cut off from both the path of her 'life' and the path of the 'great endeavour'. Her love and devotion for the great master turned first into envy and jealousy, then into blind hatred and finally insanity, which drove her to destroy her own works. She spent the last 30 years of her life in a psychiatric institute.

> No one has come further. All who raised
> their blood into a work that long took shape
> may find he can no longer hold it up;
> that it falls back to gravity, is worthless.
> For somewhere an old enmity exists
> between life and the great endeavour.

Rhythms of Life

An old man planted small apple trees.
People laughed at him and asked him:
'Why are you planting these trees?
It will be many years before they bear fruit,
And you yourself will not be able to eat them.'
The old man answered: 'I shall not harvest them.
But many years from now,
When others eat the apples from these trees
They will be grateful to me.'

Leo Tolstoy

Every life process is based on rhythm. The rhythm of a plant's growth is expansion and contraction. No living process is without this movement. Life rhythms are bound by laws of time, and these cannot be limitlessly speeded up or slowed down.

If self-actualization means development it must also obey these laws of life. One could imagine these consisting of a rhythmic alternation between two opposite directions of endeavour, with the strength of the personality acting as the central pivot. The 'two souls in our breast' that are increasingly splitting apart[89] could in this way be experienced as parts of a whole. With their potential to become mothers women are constantly being reminded that besides the pull of aspirations there is also the pull of life. This can safeguard them from being one-sided.

Finding one's own individual rhythm is part of the art of life. Others' advice will never be satisfactory here. Each woman must discover for herself what her own rhythms are, both by knowing herself and by a sense of what belongs to her destiny. Can she fill each day with a range of activities of different kinds? Or will she more easily find her way by devoting herself first of all to the vocation of running the house and bringing up her children for 10 to 20 years, and then bringing her more personal abilities to expression in suitable ways thereafter?

If you travel in the same, single direction for a very long time, however, it is important to insert *small* rhythms. Larger and smaller rhythms of life can overlap. If you are doing the same work for a great many years you sometimes need to gain distance from it. This also applies to mothers. They should have the chance now and again to do something else; go away without the children, or go to a conference. The inner distance this allows generates strength and possibly also new ideas about how to do things differently.[90]

There are a great many other life rhythms. Where a husband and wife have the same career, 'job-sharing' can be a wonderful experience if they work in unison and mutually complement one another. Other people find it more satisfactory if the two partners have quite different professions, so that in addition to their shared world they have a world of their own. It is always instructive to hear how other people do things, though one cannot copy them.

A mother who studied for a long time and had a few years in a career before her first child came says that this arrangement is the best because by that time you have to some extent fulfilled your vocational ambitions and are ready to look after your child joyfully and without restlessness. Susanna Kubelka expresses the same opinion in 'Over forty at last'[91] where she describes with great vivacity how older mothers stay young longer, are more conscious, mature and patient, and less anxious and agitated than younger women, and therefore far more cut out for bringing up children. On the other hand another mother thinks she was lucky to have her children young before she had acquired 'the taste' of professional independence. She was able to accept her motherly duties as a matter of course, was less fussy and anxious than older mothers with their first children, and did not feel the need for anything beyond motherhood until the children were 'through the worst'.

Another variation on this theme is the young woman who had difficulties choosing a profession, and maintains that it was not until she had children that she discovered meaning in her life. Whilst they were growing up, and nothing and nobody was pushing her into a vocation, she discovered her individual potential for the first time.

You cannot organize your life according to theoretical principles however often you hear them—such as that young mothers are stronger and healthier, older ones have greater maturity and life experience, etc. Some things can be planned, of course, but not many of these plans can be carried through, because life often gets in the way of our calculations.

When you have children depends to a large extent on the age at which destiny leads you to the man you wish to be their father. It also depends on the child who wants to be born at a particular time. This is something we can sense if we do not obscure this realm of existence by intellectualizing or theorizing too much.[92] It is a good thing not to regard motherhood as something that can be 'dealt with' whenever it suits us, for it does not only concern ourselves.

Here are a few examples of individual paths of destiny where life and work were in harmony. Kaethe Kruse (1883–

1968) became famous for her dolls.[93] She trained as an actress and was taking her first stage parts in Berlin when, at the age of 18, she met the sculptor Max Kruse, who was considerably older than her. She had her first child when she was 19, and the second followed shortly afterwards. Max Kruse decided that it was anathema to try to bring up children in a city such as Berlin. So they rented an old tower in Ascona, in Switzerland. Here, far away from the city, the young woman lived alone with her children, enjoying both them and nature. Their father came from Berlin from time to time to visit them. When the eldest child wished for a doll, he went from one toyshop to another in Berlin, finally writing to his young wife, saying that she would have to make a doll herself, as all the shop dolls were horribly ugly. This was the start of her career as a doll-maker. To begin with, though, she just made dolls for her own children, and she had more and more children until there were seven of them. They did not get married until after the third child was born. Eventually Max Kruse wanted to participate in family life after all, so his wife and children moved to a house on the outskirts of Berlin. One day Kaethe Kruse put some of her dolls into an exhibition of 'handmade toys'. They were immensely popular. Orders started coming in, and production gradually increased.

After the First World War, during the period of massive inflation, Max Kruse lost his fortune; and then the doll-making, which had been little more than a hobby, became a very serious business on which the family depended to keep the wolf from the door. Kaethe Kruse was 37 at the time, and had just had her seventh child. But meanwhile the eldest daughters had grown up and were a great help.

In this case, vocational work grew directly out of life. They could never have planned it this way.

Another example is the pianist Clara Schumann (1819–96) who, after the strictest training from her father, played in concerts when she was only nine.[94] Her father was violently opposed to her marriage to Robert Schumann, for he thought her calling should take precedence. The young couple fought for their love for four years, also in the courts, until they could finally marry in 1840. Clara was 21 at the time. They then shared 14 years of the most valuable creative work. During this time Clara also had eight children. The youngest was born the very same year in which Robert Schumann had to enter a psychiatric clinic because of his incurable mental illness. A few months after this the need to earn money arose, and Clara had to travel and give many concerts. Robert Schumann died two years later, and she was therefore widowed at the age of 37.

She organized her life by sending the oldest children to boarding school, a younger girl to her grandmother, and only the two youngest children stayed at home with a home help. Later on, when the eldest daughters had grown up, they looked after their little siblings. As soon as their mother could manage it financially she bought a small house in the country and here, every summer, she gathered all her children around her. In the intervals between, she kept up a correspondence with each one of them. Despite her difficult circumstances she managed to give her children a home and family life to which, as adults, they could look back with joy.

The two women whose destinies I have briefly sketched here were the kind of people who fully and totally accepted their lives as wives and mothers although they had other capacities which at a certain age they were actually forced to practise as a career. They both became mothers at a young age, and their vocation did not take priority in their lives until the end of their thirties.

One of the first women to start remonstrating against the 'lot of women' was Harriet Taylor (1809–58), the friend and later wife of John Stuart Mill, who made a name for himself in England in the nineteenth century as a philosopher, politician and author. When she was only 18, her severe and tyrannical father married her off, and she already had three children by the age of 22. Intelligent and rebellious as she was, she gathered round her a circle of friends, mainly women, who were all gifted young people. It was in this circle that John Stuart Mill met her and immediately recognized her outstanding abilities. He wrote in his auto-biography:[95]

> ... her vigorous eloquence would certainly have made her a great orator, and her profound knowledge of human nature and discernment and sagacity in practical life, would, in the times when such a carrière was open to women, have made her eminent among the rulers of mankind.

She had a profound sense of the unworthy position of women:

> In the present system of custom and opinion girls enter into what is called a contract completely ignorant of the terms of agreement, and this ignorance of theirs is con-sidered an indispensable part of their qualifications.

She had a close relationship with John Stuart Mill for 20 years, and contributed a great deal to the books he wrote.[96] As her husband tolerated their friendship, she also respected her marriage vows. Not until after his death was she granted seven years of life with Mill, dying of pneumonia at the age of 49.

We have here a very unusual life rhythm. Whereas Clara Schumann shared both her life and her work with the man she loved, Harriet Taylor's life demanded a great amount of self-discipline. She shared her life with a person she respected but did not love, and her work with someone she loved, yet she was forced for 20 long years to internalize and spiritualize her love until, at the end of her life, when she was over 40, the two streams of inner and outer life could merge. In all these examples, life brought a new beginning around the age of 40 and a period in which there was an especially intensive and wholly absorbing burst of creative energy. It seems to be a biographical law that at the mid-point of life, when energies might otherwise start to wane, we have to take hold of life anew, and then, especially in the case of women who have capacities they could not express before, they can do work of real significance. At an age when men are beginning to show signs of professional fatigue women often have large reserves of strength.

If, however, they cannot find a suitable outlet for it, this can lead to serious crises. It is often not easy for older women to find a vocation, either re-entering one they have practised before or making a new start. Here again, we see how rigid and inflexible our social forms are, for otherwise the potential that exists could be made better use of. However, opportunities often arise if people keep their eyes open and their wits about them.

Men, too, at this age, actually need the stimulus of a new start. This does not have to mean a change of vocation. What they need, at any rate, is time for self-reflection. They may hit on the idea of adopting an entirely new approach to their work, or of pursuing cultural or artistic activities in which they can be creative in a new way. The inner need to find a new impulse for the second half of life is often only a vague feeling. This can lead to a man projecting his inner problems outwards—onto his wife for instance—so that he imagines a new wife might save him the trouble of really making a new start.

It can be a terrible shock for a wife to be discarded so suddenly. All of a sudden she is alone, and will often have economic difficulties into the bargain. Yet those who do not grow embittered sometimes take admirable hold of this new situation and really make something of it. They set themselves new aims, and develop abilities in a way that might never have happened if they had stayed in the old tracks. A calamity can sometimes become an opportunity.

I am thinking here, for instance, of a woman who, after her divorce, when she was past 40, returned to her medical training which she had interrupted when she got married. She completed it and became a doctor in a clinic.

The urgent need to take up something new can hasten or trigger a process that we might not otherwise have found the courage to undertake. People have a certain instinct to stay put in a situation and to shrink from change. Holding onto motherhood as a vocation, however, has very negative consequences. Too much motherliness can make its recipients unfree and infantile. Or people get used to it and misuse it and exploit it.

It certainly takes courage to leave the security of domesticity and expose oneself to situations through which men are normally passing around the age of 30. Initial attempts at things in which one has not yet had any practice are not likely to succeed immediately. The possible mistakes tolerated in a young man in the hope that he will learn to do better are not easily overlooked in an older woman. If she does not succeed immediately she may no longer be wanted. This can easily be daunting. On the other hand, in contrast to men, whose careers are often permanent, a woman has much greater freedom to shape her life than young men, who need to succeed for existential and practical reasons. It is often easier for a married woman to work part-time, to quit a job that is not satisfying, or to take on voluntary work.[97]

Here are three basic principles that can be special guides in the life of a woman.[98] The more women realize these and can acquire recognition in a man's world, the more humanity will benefit.

The first is *being able to wait*. The tendency to leap ahead continually, to anticipate things, to force progress, has already done much harm. Self-actualization is also a matter of time, and must not be forced.

The second principle is that *success is no criterion*. Nowadays we are always hearing success praised to the skies. Of course we do not want to fail! Yet the greatest and most significant people in the past usually had very little outer or worldly success. Van Gogh did not sell a single painting during his lifetime. If you take note of biographies of this kind it becomes increasingly obvious that real human values are measured by other standards.

And the third and last principle is *the capacity for faith*. The conviction that whatever destiny brings us is the right thing for us can be a tremendous boost to our will for life. Whatever gifts we have will find an opportunity to express themselves, and if we have to renounce certain aspirations this can also be turned to gain. This thought can be of especial help to a woman who is looking for a new beginning.

These principles embody precisely the opposite of what people usually strive for nowadays. Perhaps this is also why they can offer such a source of strength, helping us to wait patiently for what life has in store for us.[99]

We must in any case dismiss the notion that creativity is inevitably associated with youth. This may have been so in earlier times, when creative work arose predominantly from natural forces. The capacities of older people are different, yet no less valuable than the gifts of the young. Conrad Ferdinand Meyer (1825–98) did practically all his work after the age of 45. Paul Cezanne (1838–1906) and Ernst Barlach (1870–1938) spent two decades in their artistic endeavours, reaping very little success until they each had a breakthrough around the age of 40—a tremendous test of patience and faith. The artistic work of Henri Matisse (1869–1954) was still undergoing important changes and development when he was over 80.[100] The list could certainly go on. It was not that such people were 'still' productive in old age, but that their productivity sprang specifically *from* the forces of age. This puts a quite different perspective on the fact that many women devote themselves principally to the care of their children and their families between the age of 20 and 40.

We said that when people are young the guiding principle in their choice of a profession ought to be: 'Where am I needed? Where can I specifically give something to the world?' In this case we look to the outside world to find ourselves. As we get older, however, the opposite gesture becomes ever more important. Personal ambitions, if we do not particularly spur them on, naturally diminish as time passes. This also enables us to examine ourselves to reflect on what capacities we have developed during our life's work and ask how we can 'realize' and round off our individuality even

more effectively? We can ascertain with increasing gratitude
that without the people we have associated with in our life
we would never have found our own identity. In looking at
our own self we find and know the world.

If you wish to know yourself,
seek yourself in the world's far breadths;
if you wish to know the world,
penetrate your inner depths.[101]

Rudolf Steiner

A Woman's Path of Schooling

> We have to take care that we do not see weakness
> in the very capacity which is our strength.
>
> *Friedrich Rittelmeyer*[102]

Having examined the potential and problems in the life of a woman from many angles, and found illustrative examples, let us return to our starting point and, referring back to the theme of the second chapter, ask why and in what respect it will contribute to the good of humanity if women find and assert themselves. This is a critical question for there are surely 'typically feminine' qualities that might *not* be desirable to see widely cultivated. 'Chattering' and 'prying' have been female stereotypes in popular literature since time immemorial, as have 'vanity' and 'jealousy'. Women have persuaded their husbands to do evil deeds at least as often as they have dissuaded them from doing so. A classic example of this is Shakespeare's Lady Macbeth. Intelligent women are often inclined to be sharp and opinionated, whereas less acute ones can lack objectivity and be swayed by their emotions. The opposite is even worse: when dull women are opinionated. We could go on.

These conventional descriptions are not mere slander on the part of a society that is hostile to women. All annoying assertions usually have a grain of truth! It can at any rate do no harm if women endeavour to observe themselves with a critical eye. Extolling everything feminine as a good in itself has no point. Is our feminine nature even the decisive aspect of our personality? One notable phenomenon of our time is the increasing prevalence of an idea, which, according to Rudolf Steiner, would come increasingly into its own in the twentieth century: the idea of reincarnation. He gave over a hundred lectures on this theme, and it is intrinsic to almost all the basic anthroposophical texts. Taking this idea seriously and learning how to live with it makes the fact of belonging to one gender suddenly less important, for in general—apart from invariable exceptions—our male and female incarnations are said to alternate. If we envisage the possibility that we ourselves—now women—could have been the very people who in former times oppressed women, whilst the oppressed were the men alive today, this does to some extent take the wind out of our sails! It can also work as a liberating thought that we are justified in thinking of ourselves in the first place as human beings, and only in second place as people who are confined within our gender's psychological and social restrictions.

Nevertheless it is true that feminine qualities should have greater status in our society, not so much because of the wishes of women alive today than because human evolution will otherwise lack balance, as is already the case. As women we should develop an awareness of the qualities we particularly need to cultivate in order to have a therapeutic effect on the world; and of other qualities, which we can well allow to slip into the background. Let us try therefore to establish a sort of model of feminine possibilities. To do this we shall have to recap a little.

We all actively engage our soul life through thinking, feeling and will, yet no one develops these three forces equally. We are familiar with the extreme opposites of the one-sided thinker and the one-sided doer. Between these two poles are those who give free rein to their feelings, and are often swayed by them. All three forces can co-exist in the most varied combinations and interplay. Everyone has their own individual blend, yet we can also distinguish typically male and typically female soul configurations. To elaborate this we will inevitably have to generalize.

Let us assume that where men are concerned feeling is less strongly developed than thinking and will, whereas for women feeling is stronger and more differentiated. This one-sidedness makes life varied and interesting, and presents no further problems provided we experience our soul life as a totality. In ordinary life, thinking leads directly to feeling and will activity; and mediated by feeling, thinking calms and orders the will.

It is however a striking fact in our time that the natural interplay of thinking, feeling and will has grown disturbed. It happens less and less naturally. The various soul forces are becoming more autonomous and disconnected.

When thinking predominates we have the philosopher who cannot grasp hold of practical life or the scientist who allows no feelings to creep in, at least not in his research field. Without permitting feelings to colour his enquiries he may think things out which, when others bring them to realization, can lead to devastating consequences. What drives him may possibly be his ambition as a scientist or his enjoyment of his own keen thinking. The latter can induce him to pursue thoughts to their final conclusions without considering in advance their results, possible consequences or secondary effects. It may be that these results and secondary effects are even well known or are written about. Yet invariably only a few people take action in response, while the general public behave as though paralysed.

The opposite does not require long explanations. Everyone knows that violence is on the increase. In its primitive form it appears as assault. But we can also include here the unscrupulous urge to power that can appear in a very subtle and concealed form, although it pervades our society. Both extremes—of thinking in isolation, and unbound will—are ubiquitous today. They are in the process of dragging civilization into the abyss.

Scientific research without ethical considerations, sealed off as it were in a thought bubble, and violence with no possibility of appealing to reason or feeling are two extreme attitudes originating from a one-sided masculinity in which either the thinking or the will have detached themselves and become isolated from the rest of soul experience.

But we cannot therefore simply jump to the conclusion that salvation will come from a more strongly developed female capacity to feel. For a start, there is a danger here too: emancipation of the life of feeling. This is no invention, for it has already become an epidemic condition: the inability to temper feelings with thought, and the risk of them erupting into spontaneous will activity. I'd like to quote Rudolf Steiner once again. In a lecture given in 1924 he said:[103]

> Feelings that have not been grasped in thought produce depression, and the only feelings that are not depressing are those which, immediately they arise, are taken hold of by the life of thought.

Depression ranks among the most common maladies of our time. Usually the first thing a psychiatrist does is to try to get a patient to bring appropriate thoughts to bear on the problem. Feelings that are worked through by thought can subsequently lead to sound will actions. If this does not happen, then they sink down into a dull, body-bound region, the so-called subconscious. This leads eventually to the unhappy condition of depression. Depressed people experience their own inner state as empty and bleak, and this is only a short step away from some form of addiction. They want to suck something into their psychological vacuum, some substance such as alcohol or drugs, or else the addictions remain entirely psychological. Particularly in the case of women a whole series of possible, very subtle addictions have been ascertained, practically all of which are connected with an unfulfilled life of feeling: an addiction to relationships, subservience, romance or sex. We speak of 'women who love too much'.[104]

Such things could not occur at all without the underlying state of consciousness that has evolved today, as we described above. The idea of love here applies only to feeling, which has broken away from soul life as a whole. Without the guidance and clarification of thought, and without activity in the sphere of vigorous will, feeling on its own leads to 'limitless dependency to the point of losing every will impulse or thought of one's own' or to 'the most pitiable state of weakness and erosion of the personality' as Rudolf Steiner described it as long ago as 1904.[105]

The sphere of feeling lies midway between our physical nature and our spiritual and mental life. On the one hand, therefore, we can have body-bound feelings that swell and escalate excessively if we do not work on them consciously. All our instincts belong in this realm, even the mother instinct. If left to themselves they can turn to perversions.[106] On the other hand there are feelings that are seated 'further up', i.e. those located closer to the spiritual, for example religious feelings. If these are not likewise filled with the clarity of thought they can degenerate into religious fanaticism and delusions. This too is not rare today, and can also be seen as a kind of addiction.

One-sided feeling is therefore just as dangerous and disordered as one-sided thinking or one-sided will. This can be a particular danger for women, and of course offers a wide field for their personal development work. The 'typical feminine vices' mentioned at the beginning are based primarily on an uncontrolled life of feeling. A sympathetic interest in others can turn into curiosity or garrulousness. Envy and hate are forms of love perverted into its opposite. Vanity and coquetry derive from a sense of beauty that has become narcissistic. To realize where one's weakness lies is the beginning of all personal development. A bit of humour goes a long way as well!

And on the other hand—as Rittelmeyer notes—we should 'take care not to see as weakness the qualities that are our particular strength', that is, our life of feeling. Feeling is the soul force that mediates between thinking and will. It has the power to reconcile and therefore acts to restore balance. We can recognize and acknowledge it without allowing it to become an end in itself—but rather let it be a kind of organ of perception which sends 'feelers' into thinking and will, to sense their qualities.

Of course there is scope here for a great many misunderstandings. When we combine thinking and feeling it is not a matter of introducing subjective feelings into scientific thinking, of colouring the latter with something illusory again. But it would be very good indeed if women could manage, in the professions and areas of life that have only been open to them during the last century, not to work as men but, distinctly and differently, as women: in other words to contribute their unique qualities and potential.

To clarify how this can be done, I will now describe three exercises, which can help support it.

1. The first offers compensating balance to counteract the undesirable way in which the life of a housewife and mother can exert a powerful pull outwards, away from her centre. It involves concentrating our thoughts.

For a certain length of time,[107] draw all your soul forces together and concentrate your whole attention on a thought you choose to think, one in fact that does not seem specially interesting to you. You can take any object, e.g. a cup, and think about it, or you can open any book and pick a sentence at random. The content matters just as little as it matters which stone you choose if you have to lift one up to train your muscles; it is a kind of training of the thought muscles. What you should be learning from this is to draw your whole awareness together into a single, focused point. This exercise has nothing to do with intelligence or knowledge. You don't need to think things about the cup that you do not know— perhaps you have never been in a china factory—just think about what you *do* know.

This exercise is a good antidote to the tiresome feeling of losing yourself in all the things of daily life, which tug at you from without and pull and push you from one activity to another. It helps develop inner forces of form and cohesion, and strengthens the personality. Without this foundation it will be much more difficult to find the strength to use your particular, individual abilities at the decisive moment.

2. The second exercise can be found in the highly recommended lecture Rudolf Steiner gave on 'Practical Training in

Thinking'.[108] He describes there how important it is to bring
the 'right feeling' to our thinking. We acquire this right
feeling by telling ourselves: 'If I can think thoughts about
things, if by means of thoughts I can find out something
about things, the thoughts must have been *in* the things to
start with. The things must actually have been constructed
according to the thoughts, for otherwise I would not be able
to draw the thoughts out of the things.'

This exercise consists in observing a process in the world,
which is ongoing and continuously accessible to us. Steiner
takes the example of the weather. You should observe it with
your full attention at a certain time of day: the cloud for-
mation, the light conditions, the wind, humidity or dryness,
etc. Turn all this into a well-formed mental image and
impress it on your memory. Do the same on the following
days, and so on. What you have to do is let one picture pass
over into the next, so that you enter the process involved in
the changing weather. An important point is not to leave out
the details, but to see the first picture as specifically and in as
much detail as possible before you transform it into the next.
You must suppress all speculation. The whole force of your
thinking is activated in perceiving attentively and trans-
forming the images. This makes thinking fluid and supple so
that it intimately inhabits objects. It turns into the kind of
thinking Goethe practised and which he called 'inscape
thinking'[109] in contrast to abstract thinking. To cultivate and
apply this kind of picture-creating thinking, which stays close
to perception, strikes me as being a specifically feminine
challenge, because women have a natural disposition for it.
This is the counterforce to abstraction, and therefore a way of
thinking that will never be achieved by computers.

You can of course practise with all kinds of other things

besides the weather; though it is important to keep to objects or phenomena drawn from nature. One possibility is to observe a plant and follow how each of its different leaf forms passes over to the next.[110] Or you can study the faces of your children at the dinner table. You will notice subtle nuances of expression all according to how they feel and the experiences they have just had. This exercise helps us to be more observant about people and situations.

3. The previous exercise provides the basis for the third, which involves developing a sense for living connections. Observe an event or action in your own life or someone else's, and instead of asking yourself whether the occurrence is painful or joyful, or right or wrong, ask yourself what part this event is playing in the biography of the person concerned. What effect does the action have on the social context and environment? To do this we likewise create a vivid picture, and thus engage in artistic activity. The exercise teaches us to experience events not in isolation but in relation to biographical and social significance. For some decisions, ascertaining the truth plays only a secondary role, while the primary one is the context in which a decision is realized. By practising this sort of thing you can eventually arrive at a direct glimpse of the possible future consequences arising from intentional actions.

Because they have a gift in this area women have always been better 'patrons' of talent. They have the knack of seeing whether a young person or a project holds promise, which deserves to be sponsored. A man's view is often distorted by being stuck too much in his own groove.

The direction in which these three exercises lead us is as follows. The focused concentration exercise helps create inner stability and tranquillity; then we turn outwards and acquire fluid mobility of thought; and finally we acquire an eye for the whole through widening our peripheral awareness.

'Holism' is an important catchword today, though people often do not know what it means. We can never achieve a holistic outlook by compiling more and more disconnected details. What is needed is a retraining of consciousness, revising our thinking in a way that affects not only 'what' but also 'how' we think. The quality of our thinking needs to change. Today, fundamentally, we still applaud and acknowledge only one kind of thinking, which we have acquired as science evolved. This is a kind of thinking, however, which is more or less void of all the feeling and will that once informed it. This is why, once it became palpably obvious how hostile it is to life's realities, people tried to instil a secondary 'ethos' into it, as a kind of add-on.

We all need a new kind of thinking, both men and women, but women have the capacity and disposition to take the lead here. This is why it seemed to me important to include this chapter.

The Bridge of the Green Snake

> What we let go of becomes our own innermost
> possession, what we hold onto slips away.
>
> *Albrecht Haushofer*

If we should ever reach a point when all human beings,
whether male or female, achieve complete social equality,
this would be connected with the fact that each of us has two
kinds of tasks: on the one hand self-actualization through
giving outward shape to our inner life; on the other hand
helpful service to our fellow human beings. It is no longer
right to assign creative tasks to some and nurturing tasks to
others, even if this difference of emphasis may persist for a
long time to come.

The achievements or work which render our personality
visible to the world are like fully grown plants. They have
reached full, visible manifestation. But like the plant, which
gives visible evidence of its stages of development, and
therefore of its past, this kind of human achievement also
points to the past. It brings something to completion. With
every created work a talent long in development—maybe
from a past life—reaches a conclusion. On the other hand,
work of the kind that involves active serving and caring for
others has a gesture that opens into the future. It does not
matter whether the work benefits me, whether I enjoy it,
whether I get something from it, or whether I can realize
myself through it and receive recognition. The individual
part of me is secondary to these tasks. Washing dishes every

day which will be used again straight away, mopping floors which will be dirtied in no time, putting children to bed night after night, caring for sick people who might never recover—all these are activities that contribute substance to the world as a whole. For centuries it was mainly women who patiently did jobs of this kind, making their will-power available to the world in an unselfish way. Many artisan and mechanical jobs also belong in this category, even work on the assembly line; everything that does not give personal satisfaction but is detached from one's personality, so that one cannot immediately experience oneself through it. These jobs are like seeds, which will only come to fruition and maturity in the future. Performed conscientiously and tenaciously over and over again, they give rise to a maturity of will, which one clearly recognizes in older mothers of many children, and in workmen, but which is hard to put into words. In all religious orders the monks and the nuns were given menial tasks to do in addition to their inner work.

In his lectures on the karma of vocation, Rudolf Steiner points out that Jakob Boehme's capacity to write mystical books had its origin in the distant past, and brought something to a conclusion. But the fact that he was also a shoemaker, working for his fellow human beings, was the seed for something that would only come into effect in the far future, in later incarnations. Rudolf Steiner says:[111]

There is something very remarkable about this, for it hints at the fact that we often attach so little value to certain things in earthly life only because they are the starting point for something we shall only value in the future. It is natural that people's inner nature is far more intimately connected with the past. They are therefore often far less fond of something that represents a beginning than of what comes to them from the past.

We are much more conscious of the past than of the future; in fact we might even say that we are asleep in everything relating to the future:

> Thus human beings are really deeply unconscious with regard to the whole context into which they enter when they adopt a profession. Through this profession—not what they enjoy about it but through what develops without their full awareness—arises value for the future.[112]

So it is understandable that people's evaluations are not always correct, for, as Steiner says in the same context, 'the greatest achievements are a conclusion, and the most menial tasks are always a beginning'.

If we read European fairy tales and try to interpret the message they still have for people of our time, we can be struck by the significant role of the simpleton, or the boy who sits in the ashes, or the poor, industrious girl Cinderella. Many people will admit this only very reluctantly. In feminist circles fairy tales have been discredited or subverted precisely because of figures such as Cinderella. It looks too much like a didactic attempt to fit children into a certain role from childhood onwards. In America the 'Cinderella complex' was coined to label women who cannot free themselves from subservience. Some women might have this problem, but the expression indicates a lack of knowledge of fairy tales. For there are plenty of stories—mainly from Russia and Scandinavia—where it is, equally, a male figure who sits in the ashes and has to do menial tasks. Cinderella is a figure who distinguishes herself from her sisters principally by her sense for things that are alive and growing. She does not ask her father for treasure, jewellery or clothes (no salary rise or success). All she asks for is a simple hazel twig, which she plants and then tends every day. And so it grows into a tree:

> Cinderella went to it three times a day, wept and prayed, and each time a little white bird flew onto the tree. If she uttered a wish the little bird dropped down to her what she had wished for.[113]

Thus, through a life of contemplation that includes both active service and patient waiting, a relationship is built up with the 'little white birds', the doves. We may see this as a soul quality which Cinderella develops and later on uses to distinguish the seeds which will germinate from the bad ones that are no longer fertile. She is preparing for the future, which is why she is so modest, and her sisters do not like her at all. In her we see clearly that we 'so little value certain things in earthly life only because they are the starting point for something we shall only value in the future'. Cinderella also knows that it is a question of finding a balance between two opposing spheres of existence. She manages to call a halt at the height of her 'success' and return to the ashes. She has a masterly grasp of the swinging or rocking principle, the control of life rhythms. This is clearly the precondition for her eventual rise to the position of queen.

Cinderella is an archetypal representative of one aspect of feminine nature. There is, however, another side, which is the polar opposite. This is the 'princess on the glass mountain', the 'king's daughter of the golden roof', the 'princess from the castle of the golden sun', 'the fairest of the fair', or whatever else she may be called.[114] Here we have a feminine figure who from the very beginning is outstanding for her radiant, sunlike beauty. Her fame spreads throughout the world, and one prince after the other sets out to win her. But such female beings are as far from the earth as Cinderella is close to it. They live in a distant and inaccessible realm, on an island in the ocean or on 'the glass mountain'. Other mountains may be hard to climb; a glass mountain is virtually impossible to ascend.

These princesses have to wait until they are won; they themselves cannot contribute much towards it. They are as it were purely symbols, representing radiant spirituality detached from any will element. This is why they are so passive. They are untouchable but desirable: the virginal, love-awakening power of wisdom.

These two opposing archetypes are to be found in every woman, and we can feel them within ourselves. The power of wisdom just described shows itself in them as a feeling of long knowing things intuitively which men have to work hard for. Yet this foreknowledge is often difficult to grasp. If we want to take hold of it we slip about as though we were on a glass mountain. It hovers above the earth and causes women generally to be closer to spiritual matters than men. Yet on the other hand they are also often more practical. The Cinderella part of them keeps them more down to earth, so that they can stay in touch with their common sense.

From this point of view it is very illuminating to read John Stuart Mill's descriptions in his biography of his friend Harriet Taylor, mentioned in the previous chapter. He writes:[115]

Alike in the highest regions of speculation and in the smaller practical concerns of daily life, her mind was the same perfect instrument, piercing to the very heart and marrow of the matter; always seizing the essential idea or principle.

He describes her contribution to his writing in the following way:

What was abstract and purely scientific was generally mine; the properly human element came from her: in all that concerned the application of philosophy to the exigencies of human society and progress, I was her pupil, alike in boldness of speculation and cautiousness of practical judgment. For, on the one hand, she was much more courageous and far-sighted than without her I should have been, in anticipations of an order of things to come, in which many of the limited generalizations now so often confounded with universal principles will cease to be applicable. Those parts of my writings, and especially of the Political Economy, which contemplate possibilities in the future such as, when affirmed by Socialists, have in general been fiercely denied by political economists, would, but for her, either have been absent, or the suggestions would have been made much more timidly and in a more qualified form. But while she thus rendered me bolder in speculation on human affairs, her practical turn of mind, and her almost unerring estimate of practical obstacles, repressed in me all tendencies that were really visionary. Her mind invested all ideas in a concrete shape, and formed to itself a conception of how they would actually work: and her knowledge of the existing feelings and conduct of mankind was so seldom at fault, that the weak point in any unworkable suggestion seldom escaped her.[116]

In this characterization the possibilities and qualities of specifically feminine thinking are portrayed very pertinently! When Margarete Mitscherlich argues that 'the future is feminine or it does not exist'[117] this cannot mean that as many women as possible should get into leading positions. If they do so by retaining the prevailing masculine way of thinking we shall not get any further. The point is that feminine thinking, feminine spirituality, as we showed in the previous chapter, must penetrate our culture more and more, unless 'culture' is soon to become an empty phrase.

Many people feel this need, which has resulted recently in the founding of a 'spiritual women's movement' in America and Europe.[118] Unfortunately people are rather in the dark about what 'feminine spirituality' really is. It seems too easy to suggest drawing on eastern traditions to revive ancient feminine powers. This, however, is what is being proposed in some quarters, even if it is given a more scientific gloss for modern times. When we are told that we should use intuition, symbolism and even magic, and no longer think simply in a rational, analytical manner, this is a kind of mystification. It hearkens back to the past and will have little power to sustain the future. Neither will we make any progress if we wax ecstatic and appeal directly to our feelings without combining these with thinking and will. Here lurks the danger of sentimentality.

We should instead try to connect with the kind of thinking typified by Harriet Taylor, who combined in an unusually harmonious way 'bold speculation' with 'a practical turn of mind'. What gave her the capacity to bridge these two extremes? Harriet Taylor was a child of the nineteenth century, which had very different qualities from ours, and she therefore possessed a sense of morality which gave her a secure foundation. John Stuart Mill speaks of her again as follows in his autobiography:

> Her intellectual gifts did but minister to a *moral character* at once the noblest and the best balanced which I have ever met with in life. Her unselfishness was not that of a taught system of duties, but of a heart, which thoroughly identified itself with the feelings of others, and often went beyond this in consideration for them by imaginatively investing their feelings with the intensity of her own. A passion for justice might have been thought to be her strongest feeling, but for her boundless generosity and a lovingness ever ready to pour itself forth upon any or all human beings who were capable of giving the smallest feeling in return.

It was thanks to the foundation of this 'moral character' that she became neither a fanatic nor a dry and theoretical social reformer. Much as we may admire such a character, we no longer have access to the disposition of soul it implies. In our century we have to find another bridge. And maybe we can seek help once again in a fairy-tale image.

Goethe, too, wrote a fairy tale, one of the few literary fairy tales whose authentic symbolic imagery is equal to that of folk tales. This is true also of the way in which it points far into the future. Its theme is the harmonizing of two human faculties represented by figures in whom we can recognize the two feminine prototypes we have already identified in Cinderella and the princess on the glass mountain. Of course, every 'picture' worthy of the name can be seen from a wide variety of aspects. We are, however, perfectly entitled to choose a particular interpretation that most echoes our needs. In Goethe's fairy tale the two chief feminine characters are called the green snake and the beautiful lily.[119] They live in two realms separated by a river. This river can be crossed only under very special circumstances. In his fairy tale Goethe wanted to present in imaginative form something that Schiller treated philosophically in his *Letters on the Aesthetic Education of Man*. There he speaks of two opposing human impulses, one coming from the material realm and the other from the realm of form; one could also say the 'sensual' and the 'spiritual' principles. There is a wide gulf between them, and it is time they were reconnected. The green snake in Goethe's fairy tale corresponds to the material drive. She is closely connected with the earthy, sense-perceptible world. She crawls through rocky chasms and clings to the mineral realm. As a snake she lives in the horizontal plane and can only partially raise herself, but she can wind her whole body around things and sense their being. This is a very similar picture to the one we mentioned earlier, where elemental love and mother instinct are depicted in the folk tale of the green mermaid (see page 79). The beautiful lily on the other bank of the river, in contrast, is a pure and regal virgin living in a great garden with magnificent trees. But the plants in this garden bear neither blossoms nor fruit, and the maiden is as inaccessible as the princess on the glass mountain. She seems to be under a curse: every living being she touches dies. If we see in her the 'form' impulse, i.e. the purely spiritual principle, it is clear that everything sensual is repelled by her because, initially, the sensual and the spiritual have to be seen as two mutually exclusive principles. The beautiful lily's untouchable nature is very painful to her, especially after the young man who loves her falls dead to the ground in a desperate attempt to embrace her.

Both worlds, on either aside of the river, lack something.

How can they be brought into a connection with one another?

After many years of intense study of Goethe's fairy tale, Rudolf Steiner based his first Mystery Drama on it, *The Portal of Initiation*.[120] He has, so to say, updated the fairy tale and transposed it into another art form. But the characters and the action correspond so closely that they can illuminate one another. In the first draft of his drama Rudolf Steiner even kept the names used in Goethe's fairy tale. As we saw, there are two characters, Snake and Lily. In later versions they received individual names: the lily was 'Maria' and the snake 'the other Maria'. No doubt Rudolf Steiner was suggesting that these are two aspects of the same being.

Maria is a woman who, in her spiritual development, far surpasses those around her. Yet there is a painful mystery in her life: the very people whom she specially loves and is loved by—her friend Johannes Thomasius and her foster child—cannot blossom in her presence; their development stagnates. She feels completely merged with the cosmos and the truth but she realizes that she finds it more and more impossible to work in the material world, that the tie that binds spirit and matter together is growing ever thinner. She knows that this thread must not break completely.

Rudolf Steiner portrays this as an anticipation in Maria's destiny of something that humankind as a whole is experiencing in the epoch which began in the twentieth century. Millions will feel—so he says—what Maria is painfully perceiving as a gulf dividing her from other people, but they will not realize what it means: the birth pangs of a new age in which old human capacities have to be lost because new forces are being born.[121]

This is more than a psychological problem. The play

addresses the possibility that modern people will become increasingly aware of impressions coming from the spiritual world, even without spiritual training. This is indeed becoming more frequent today, especially among younger people. The loosening of soul and spirit from matter that makes this possible is the result of an abstract thinking which has long been practised in our culture. 'Abstraction' means 'being drawn away from'. In other words, in the process of abstraction the spiritual is 'drawn away from' the material. This can lead to a rupture of the link between spirit and matter or, in other words, to abstract thinking no longer finding access to reality. We could accuse such thinking of being 'masculine'. In reality we are all in the grip of it, men and women alike, and it is vital today that we see the danger that lurks in it and try consciously to prevent it.

In Rudolf Steiner's drama, Maria is a representative of modern humanity and consciously experiences what in most people is only a vague feeling. We have here a predicament without an easy remedy. According to Goethe's fairy tale, help must first come from another direction. The princess on the glass mountain must wait until somebody climbs it, and the beautiful lily must wait until the bridge has been built from the other bank of the river. This requires something that has a central significance in the fairy tale: the sacrifice of the snake. The 'other Maria', who in Rudolf Steiner's drama corresponds to the green snake, is a woman who has lived fully through motherhood. Her warmth of heart gave her the strength to bring up her children as capable human beings, even when she had to do it on her own after premature death deprived her of her husband. Subsequently she works as a nurse, and continuously receives new vitality through a spiritual world-view to which she is devoted with religious intensity. She is called 'Maria's humble sister', and serves the reflection of the spiritual in the physical. In a scene in the elemental world she appears as a shining snakelike figure and describes her own actions in the following words:

> I struggle my way through rocky depths
> And try to clothe in human words
> The rock's own will;
> I sense earth being,
> And wish to think within the human head
> The earth's own thinking.
> I drink pure living air,
> And air's powers I transform
> Into human feeling.

The way in which she speaks of rocks, earth and air makes it clear that we are dealing with a force that is elemental, i.e. an instinctive human force in the best sense of the word. We have already discussed this in the chapter on the mother instinct. The other Maria works out of a motherly instinct of helping, comforting and caring for other people—which is precisely what is denied to Maria.

Rudolf Steiner chiefly addresses the social side of the problem in a way that is initially unusual and surprising: if each of the two women wishes to stay as she is, she will not only hinder her own development but also that of the other. Each must make a sacrifice to allow further development.

To begin with, the sacrifice of the other Maria is required—again closely following the action of Goethe's fairy tale. If she decides to strive consciously rather than only absorbing the spiritual through feeling, as something that endows her with strength, she will enable her higher sister to become active in the material realm. Only by adding the light of consciousness to the warmth of her love can she give warmth to Maria's light of love and pave the way for her to connect with the earth.

How is this to happen? In Goethe's fairy tale the green snake devours the gold coins which the will-o'-the-wisps throw to her. In these latter we can see representatives of intellectual thought. Intellect is brilliant and mobile. It churns out thoughts like the minting of coins, and does not care what happens to them afterwards. The snake eats the coins and digests them. They melt in her body and make it glow from within. Intellectual thoughts acquire a different quality when they are 'digested'; they can bring light into areas that previously were shrouded in dark, in the life of instinct, just as the snake brings light into the rocky crevices. When clear thinking penetrates into instinctive soul life then 'the time has come'. This is a key word in Goethe's fairy tale, and the goal to which the path of training described in the previous chapter also leads. When instinct is enlightened by thinking it is no longer instinct. It is transformed into the light-filled power of thought. The snake sacrifices herself, i.e. she ceases to exist as a snake and crumbles into a heap of shining jewels.

We have already seen that naturally endowed mother instincts are growing ever weaker and may disappear altogether. They are crumbling like the green snake. Will they simply vanish without trace? The snake does not do that. The product of her decomposition takes the form of jewels. In Goethe's fairy tale a great deal depends on these jewels not being left lying around as rubbish but being carefully gathered up and thrown into the river. Out of them arises the majestic bridge, which henceforth connects the two separate realms with one another.

If the stones had been left lying around, the snake's

sacrifice would have been in vain. The creative strength of instinct which people have poured into world evolution for centuries would then prove useless. The force of instinct would still break down, but without being transformed. There would be evidence of decadence, as is already the case.

What does this mean? We should not let what we still possess as the vestiges and transformed fruit of mother love seep away. We should not dismiss it with contempt, but incorporate it into the stream of life. We need the snake's power, yet rather than reanimating it we must metamorphose it to overcome the abstract nature of our culture.

The abstract hostility to life that exists today can be reconnected with living necessities when enough women know that they need to use the jewels of their specifically feminine qualities for building the bridge which can link the spiritual with the sense realm.

And so we come to the other aspect of the matter. When the bridge has been built through the sacrifice of the snake, the lily has to set out on the path that actually enters the realm of earthly life. She has to leave her garden paradise and go to meet the snake. The garden of the beautiful lily is the realm of pure spirit. No earthly fruits ripen there. The realm of abstract thought cannot be directly applied to earth existence.

Let us look at a specific, somewhat simplified example of this. When we realize that our instincts do not tell us any more—say, how to bring up our children—we turn to books for help. There we find intellectual presentations of things that may be absolutely right. They make sense to us and we want to put them into practice. Sooner or later we will notice that this is a fruitless undertaking. The child in the book is not our child. It is certainly necessary to penetrate life's questions with thinking, and to seek advice. But when it comes to real action we must forget what we have read and go to the realm of the green snake to *learn to see* in her way.

Only if we really observe our child will we see what is needed. But then we should act on our findings. To go the way of the snake means to be guided neither by set rules nor by personal feelings of pleasure or displeasure, but by what we perceive to be the objective reality.

In his second Mystery Play, *The Soul's Probation*, Rudolf Steiner compares the sacrifice of Maria with that of the 'other Maria'. Despite or maybe precisely because of her outstanding spiritual qualities, Maria is shown as not being free of 'intellectual vanity' and 'self-conceit'. She applies these words to herself when she takes herself to task. She had a great influence, a good one, on her friend, the painter Johannes Thomasius. But she has to realize that this influence gave her a certain satisfaction and tied him down. He loved this bondage, and he is hurt when he feels her growing reticence. She nevertheless brings herself to hold back and to moderate her need for recognition, however refined and subtle it may have been. There is no call for an outward dissolution of their friendship, only for an inwardly more tolerant stance.

> *Maria:* In future I will not interpret
> Too quickly knowledge from the spirit realm.
> I will esteem it as a power
> To form my soul—not as instruction
> Through which I can be spared the trouble
> To learn in life itself the aims for action.[122]

Not even the 'knowledge from the spirit realm', in this case Maria's recognition of her deep feeling of karmic connection with her friend, must become the direct motive for action.

We have to learn to act out of the requirements of the situation and then grasp the 'whole picture'.

The two qualities represented by the 'one' and the 'other' Maria have first to be developed separately, by turns, before they can unite in one individual. One path leads from dull, unconscious vitality to clear, waking consciousness. The other leads from the realm of pure spirituality in thinking, which is however hostile to life, across the bridge into detailed work for the benefit of humankind. This is the path of 'learning from life itself the aims for action'.

All human beings, whether women or men, can strive to advance on this path in an individual way to the extent that their circumstances allow, and thus build a healing and wholesome future.

Notes

1. Ingrid Riedel: *Tabu im Märchen*, Olten 1985.
2. This is Rudolf Steiner's own formulation in § 1 of the Statutes of the General Anthroposophical Society, from Christmas 1923.
3. Rudolf Steiner, *Zur Geschichte und aus den Inhalten der ersten Abteilung der Esoterischen Schule 1904–1914*. English edition: *From the History and Contents of the First Section of the Esoteric School 1904–1914*, Anthroposophic Press, 1998.
4. Florence Herve (ed.), *Geschichte der deutschen Frauenbewegung*, Cologne 1987.
5. *Die Philosophie der Freiheit*, Berlin 1894. English edition: *The Philosophy of Freedom*, Rudolf Steiner Press, 1979.
6. Jeffrey Moussaieff Masson, *The Assault on Truth: Freud's Suppression of the Seduction Theory*, Farrar Straus & Giroux, 1984. Masson's publication caused an uproar and scandal in the world of psychoanalysis. He was dismissed from his post at the Freud Archive. Alice Miller before him (1981) experienced something similar, as did Freud's pupil and friend Sandor Ferenczi as far back as 1932; towards the end of his life he returned to his teacher's 'seduction theory' and was ostracized by the scientific community.
7. For more on the nature of masculine and feminine qualities, see Signe Schaefer, Betty Staley, Margli Matthews, *Ariadne's Awakening*, Hawthorn Press, 1986.
8. Der Demokratische Frauenbund Deutschlands or DFD.
9. Betty Friedan, *The Second Stage*, Abacus, 1983.
10. Translation of all Rilke quotes in this book are by M. Barton.
11. Rudolf Steiner, lecture of 21 December 1916, 'Christmas at a Time of Grievous Destiny', in: *The Festivals and their Meaning*, Rudolf Steiner Press, 2002.
12. Ulrich Mann, 'Minoische Tragödie. Kretas Geschichte und Kult als dramatisches Geschehen', in: *Antaios*, vol. 4, no. 3, September 1962, eds Mircea Eliade and Ernst Jünger.
13. Johannes Heymann Mathwich, *Geheimnis der Mütter*, privately printed.

14. Adalbert Stifter, *Der fromme Spruch*, Wiesbaden 1959.

15. Quoted by Erich Fromm in: *The Art of Loving*, Perennial,1989.

16. Alice Schwarzer, *Simone de Beauvoir Today: Conversations, 1972–1982*, Hogarth Press, 1984.

17. In: Katherine Mansfield, *Bliss, and Other Stories*, Alfred A. Knopf, 1920.

18. Rainer Maria Rilke, *Briefe*, Frankfurt a/M 1966, letter no. 24 dated 14 May 1904 to Franz Xaver Kappus, published in English in *Letters to a Young Poet*, W. W. Norton, 1993.

19. Thornton Wilder, *The Alcestiad, or A Life in the Sun*, Harper Collins, 1979.

20. Rosa Mayreder, *Geschlecht und Kultur*, Vienna 1923.

21. Mariam Bâ, *Ein so langer Brief. Ein afrikanisches Frauenschicksal*, Frankfurt a/M—Berlin 1988.

22. Rudolf Steiner, *Briefe*, Vol. II: 1890–1925.

23. Friedrich Schaller, 'Sexualität' in: *Naturwissenschaftliche Rundschau*, January 1989.

24. Peter Handke, *Kindergeschichte*, Frankfurt a/M 1981.

25. Sheila Kitzinger, *Women as Mothers*, HarperCollins, 1978.

26. Quoted by Stefan Leber in: *Geschlechtlichkeit und Erziehungsauftrag*, Stuttgart 1981, 1989.

27. Felicitas Betz, *Märchen als Schlüssel zur Welt*, Lahr 1977.

28. Heide Göttner-Abendroth, *Die Göttin und ihr Heros*, Munich 1980.

29. Susanna Kubelka, *Endlich über vierzig. Der reifen Frau gehört die Welt*, Zurich 1981.

30. Ernst Barlach, *Die Dramen*, Munich/Zurich 1985.

31. *The Kalevala: Or the Land of Heroes*, translation by William Forsell Kirby, Society of Metaphysicians, 1996.

32. This and the next three quotations are taken from Otakar Nahodil: 'Mysterien heiliger Mutterschaft. Zur Archäologie des "Matriarchats"', in: Gerd-Klaus Kaltenbrunner (ed.), *Mutterschaft*, Munich 1987.

33. In: *Bulgarische Volksmärchen*, Düsseldorf/Cologne 1971, no. 23: 'Das ungeborene Mädchen'.

34. Erich Neumann, *Ursprünge des Bewusstseins*, Zurich 1949.

35. Johann Jakob Bachofen, *Das Mutterrecht*, Basel 1861.

36. 'Der Jüngling und das grosse Tier mit dem Menschenkopf' from: *Der Mann in allen Farben, Märchen aus der Gascoigne*, vol. 1, Stuttgart 1977.
37. Elisabeth Badinter, *Mutterliebe—Geschichte eines Gefühls vom siebzehnten Jahrhundert bis heute*, Munich 1984.
38. Hans Wollschläger, *Karl May. Grundriss eines gebrochenen Lebens*, Zurich 1976.
39. Cf. the interviews in Alice Schwarzer's book *Simone de Beauvoir Today: Conversations, 1972–1982*, Hogarth Press, 1984.
40. Editor's note: While such desire is nowadays strongly overlaid and concealed by the sexualization of every aspect of life, this statement is probably true nevertheless.
41. 'Marienkind', no. 3 in the Grimms' collection of tales.
42. 'Bei der schwarzen Frau', in: *Deutsche Märchen aus dem Donauland*, Dusseldorf/Cologne 1958.
43. Ingrid Riedel, *Tabu im Märchen*, Olten 1985.
44. Ingrid Riedel, op. cit.
45. Cf. Susanna Kubelka on late sexual maturity, in: *Endlich über vierzig*, Zurich 1981.
46. In her booklet *Ich will ins Haus zurück* (Munich 1979), Christiane Collange describes research which very clearly demonstrates the different disposition of men and women. The researcher found that men's pupils expand when they see photos of beautiful, naked women, even if they showed no other reaction. Women responded in this way neither to photos of men, whether clothed or naked, nor to couples, nor women. Only when they were shown pictures of young children did their pupils expand.
47. Cf. Flensburger Sonderheft no. 1, 1987: *Partnerschaft und Ehe*.
48. In hundreds of works of art, painters and sculptors have portrayed the idealized, usually youthful female body. There were few women artists among them. But those there were (e.g. Käthe Kollwitz, Paula Modersohn-Becker) did not primarily depict men but also women, though in a less idealized form and very often as mothers.
49. Editor's note: Likewise, one can say that children grow 'down' into their limbs and earthly life as much as they grow *up*.
50. Editor's note: This may, increasingly, be a debatable point. Though

perhaps still generally true, there are many men who nowadays take at least an equal share in this area.

51. Editor's note: Besides traditional church weddings, there are, of course, all sorts of possible ceremonies, both religious and not, which mark the joining of two people in marriage, and can have a similar 'consciousness-raising' effect.

52. See further in Evelyn Capel and Tom Ravetz, *Seven Sacraments in the Christian Community*, Floris Books, 1999.

53. Adalbert Stifter, *Feldblumen*, 1841.

54. At Dornach, near Basel, Switzerland.

55. For more on reincarnation, particularly in relation to gender, see also the chapter in this volume 'A Woman's Path of Schooling'.

56. Rudolf Steiner, *Das Prinzip der spirituellen Ökonomie*, lecture of 7 June 1909.

57. Dietrich Bauer, Max Hoffmeister, Hartmut Görg, *Children who Communicate Before they are Born*, Temple Lodge Publishing, 2005.

58. Cf. Maria Christiane Benning, *Merlin der Zauberer und König Artus*, Ahrweiler 1958.

59. I found this poem amongst my father's papers after his death and unfortunately do not know who the author is.

60. Therese Schröer, *Über praktische Kindererziehung*, Stuttgart 1958.

61. Editor's note: This is of course not to say that, in the case of the death or absence of a mother, this role cannot be filled by another to some extent, or even very well. But the natural and deep connection a mother has with her child can be extremely hard to replicate without enormous dedication and love.

62. There are many suggestions relating to family life, alternative forms of education and ways of relating to children in the book *Lifeways* by Gudrun Davy and Bons Voors, Hawthorn Press, 1996.

63. Anne Morrow Lindbergh, *Gift from the Sea*, Pantheon, 1991.

64. Editor's note: It will be clear by now that the author does, rightly, ascribe certain qualities to women which men cannot easily replicate. In the twenty-first century, however, some years after this book was first published in German, it seems only right to emphasize that men do succeed in taking over many such roles, and develop their feminine side. Perhaps this simply requires a much

greater degree of consciousness and therefore comes less naturally— but this is not to say it cannot be done. In this sense, references to 'the mother' in this book should not be understood as an absolutely exclusive domain of women alone.

65. Report on the work of Claudia Schmidt, in: *Sprachreport* (1/87) published by the Institut für deutsche Sprache, Mannheim.

66. Editor's note: Hawthorn Press, Stroud, publishes a good range of 'festivals' books with a wealth of ideas and activities for celebrating seasonal festivals from all traditions.

67. Matthias Claudius, *Werke*, Dresden, no year of publication given.

68. Editor's note: The 'slow food' movement has recently come to wider attention, and promotes very similar ideas of a less hasty lifestyle.

69. Doris Reim (ed.), *Frauen berichten vom Kinderkriegen*, Munich 1984.

70. *Die kleine Chronik der Anna Magdalena Bach*, Leipzig 1931.

71. Rosa Mayreder, *A Survey of the Woman Problem*, Hyperion Press, 1993.

72. Editor's note: No judgement is intended here on women who decide not to have children: every destiny is unique, and each person will of course make their own free decisions to best fulfil themselves and their potential.

73. One example of this among many can be found in: Maxie Wander, *Leben wär' eine prima Alternative*, Berlin 1979.

74. Editor's note: For details of these and other, similar meditation exercises, see Warren Lee Cohen, *Raising the Soul*, Sophia Books, 2006.

75. On the benefit of telling rather than reading stories, see Nancy Mellon, *Storytelling with Children*, Hawthorn Press, 2000.

76. In this connection, see Horst Kornberger, *Story Medicine*, School of Integral Art, Australia, 2007; and, Susan Perrow, *Healing Stories for Challenging Behaviour*, Hawthorn Press, 2008.

77. Rilke, 'Requiem', op. cit.

78. Editor's note: There is of course no hard-and-fast rule or dogma about this. As parents we can remain finely tuned to what our children are doing, especially if we sense they may be putting themselves at risk. How we intervene or refrain from doing so is a matter for each parent's individual judgement, but current wisdom

holds that good communication, developed from the earliest years, will go a long way to keeping our youngsters in—even unspoken—dialogue with us.

79. Therese Schröer, *Über praktische Kindererziehung*, Hamburg 1873.
80. Anne Morrow Lindbergh, *Hour of Gold, Hour of Lead. Diaries and Letters 1929–1932*, Harvest/HBJ, 1993.
81. The title of a famous essay by Virginia Woolf.
82. Rosa Mayreder, *A Survey of the Woman Problem*, Hyperion Press, 1993.
83. These and the next three quotes are from: Doris Reim (ed.), *Frauen berichten vom Kinderkriegen*, Munich 1984.
84. Rudolf Steiner: *Das Karma des Berufes des Menschen in Anknüpfung an Goethes Leben*. English edition: *The Karma of Vocation*, Anthroposophic Press, 1984.
85. Kathleen Ferrier, *Her Life and a Memoir*, Penguin, 1962.
86. This and the following quotation come from: Rainer Maria Rilke, *Briefe*, Frankfurt a/M 1966, letter no. 331 to Countess M.
87. Rainer Maria Rilke, Requiem für Paula Modersohn-Becker.
88. Anne Delbee, *Der Kuss. Kunst und Leben der Camille Claudel*, Munich 1985.
89. This is a reference to a line in Goethe's *Faust*.
90. For an account of a long pilgrimage by a woman, which had a profound effect on her life and outlook (although this was after her children left home), see: Karin Jarman, *Touching the Horizon*, Temple Lodge, 2008.
91. Susanna Kubelka, *Endlich uber Vierzig*, Droemer Knaur, 2001.
92. Here I would like to refer the reader once again to the book, mentioned in note 57, *Children who Communicate Before they are Born* (in the chapter 'The Gateway to Motherhood'). This offers a unique perspective on these aspects.
93. Cf. Käthe Kruse, *Ich und meine Puppen*, Freiburg 1982.
94. Cf. Eugenie Schumann, *Erinnerungen*, Stuttgart 1925.
95. John Stuart Mill, *Autobiography*, Penguin Classic, 1989.
96. In his autobiography, Mill mentions several books which he worked on together with Harriet. Her 'disinclination for all publicity' prevented him from properly acknowledging her input. *The*

Subjection of Women was only published after her death, and became an essential text for the women's movement.

97. Editor's note: This evidently refers to more old-fashioned circumstances where the husband is the chief breadwinner. Many women, particularly single mothers—unless they are on benefits, which can prove a different kind of trap—now find themselves having to work for reasons that are as practical and essential as men. Many households have also of course become reliant on two incomes to fund a family's lifestyle. In all such phenomena we increasingly see the role and gender divisions crumbling, bringing both problems and opportunities as the author highlights.

98. Rudolf Steiner describes these three principles as those of the genuine Rosicrucians of former times. See Rudolf Steiner, *The East in the Light of the West*, Garber Communications, 1986.

99. Editor's note: Waiting patiently need not, of course, mean abject submission and subjection. Rather, such a stance preserves the individual's true sense of her potential as she bides her time until she can act or take the necessary steps. A writer whom the author quotes elsewhere, Ann Morrow Lindbergh, writes in *Gift From the Sea*: 'The sea does not reward those who are too anxious, too greedy, or too impatient. To dig for treasures shows not only impatience and greed, but lack of faith. Patience, patience, patience, is what the sea teaches. Patience and faith. One should lie empty, open, choiceless as a beach—waiting for a gift from the sea.'

100. Almut Bockemühl, 'Kunst als Schöpfung aus Alterskräften. Henri Matisse und die "Chapelle du Rosaire" in Venice', in the journal *Die Drei*, November 1988.

101. Rudolf Steiner, *Finding the Greater Self. Meditations for Harmony and Healing*, Sophia Books, 2002.

102. Friedrich Rittelmeyer, *Einene leuchtenden Kern im Inneren schaffen. Aphorismen zur Selbsterziehung*, Stuttgart 1992.

103. Rudolf Steiner, *Education for Special Needs*, lecture of 28 June 1924, Rudolf Steiner Press, 1998.

104. The title of a well-known book by Robin Norwood, Pocket, 1990.

105. Rudolf Steiner, *Knowledge of Higher Worlds*, Rudolf Steiner Press, 1963.

106. Editor's note: This is much more likely in modern societies where communities are no longer bound by accepted beliefs, rituals and moral codes. In the past, and still today in ethnic tribes, such values and traditions helped keep impulses, instincts and emotions within proper and healthy limits.

107. Editor's note: five minutes may be sufficient, and 15 or 20 minutes probably ideal. See also Warren Lee Cohen, *Raising the Soul*, Sophia Books, 2006.

108. Rudolf Steiner, lecture of 18 January 1909. Published in *Anthroposophy in Everyday Life*, Anthroposophic Press, 1995.

109. Editor's note: This word comes of course from Gerard Manley Hopkins who postdates Goethe. The word Goethe used in German is 'gegenständliches Denken' which means, roughly, 'thinking within the object'.

110. See Margaret Colquhoun, *New Eyes for Plants*, Hawthorn Press, 1996.

111. Rudolf Steiner, *The Karma of Vocation*, op. cit.

112. Ibid.

113. No. 21 in the collection of fairy tales by the Brothers Grimm.

114. For instance in the Grimms' story 'Faithful John' or the Norwegian fairy tale 'The Princess on the Glass Mountain'.

115. John Stuart Mill, *Autobiography*, Penguin Classic, 1989.

116. Ibid.

117. Margarete Mitscherlich, *Die Zunkunft ist weiblich*, Zurich 1987.

118. Cf. Hallie Iglehardt, *Weibliche Spiritualität*, Munich 1987, or Heide Göttner-Abendroth, *Die Göttin und ihr Heros*, Munich 1980. On the other hand, a view of feminine spirituality that also calls on the forces of thinking and consciousness can be found in: Signe Schaefer, Betty Staley, Margli Matthews, *Ariadne's Awakening, Taking Up the Threads of Consciousness*, Hawthorn Press, 1986.

119. J. W. von Goethe, *The Green Snake and the Beautiful Lily*, Hawthorn Press, 2000.

120. Rudolf Steiner, *Four Mystery Dramas*, Rudolf Steiner Press, 1998.

121. Rudolf Steiner, *Entwürfe, Fragmente und Paralipomena zu den vier Mysteriendramen.*

122. Rudolf Steiner, *Four Mystery Dramas*, Rudolf Steiner Press, 1998.

ALSO IN THE 'BRINGING SPIRIT TO LIFE' SERIES:

Time for Transformation, Through Darkness to the Light
Margarete van den Brink and Hans Stolp

Under the Sky, Playing, Working and Enjoying Adventures in the Open Air, A Handbook for Parents, Carers and Teachers
Sally Schweizer

Understand Your Temperament!, A Guide to the Four Temperaments
Gilbert Childs

Well I Wonder . . ., Childhood in the Modern World, A Handbook for Parents, Carers and Teachers
Sally Schweizer

Your Reincarnating Child, Welcoming a Soul to the World
Gilbert Childs and Sylvia Childs